Visit Cram101.com for full Practice Exams

Just The facts101
Textbook Key Facts

Textbook Outlines, Highlights, and Practice Quizzes

Essentials of Sociology

by Anthony Giddens, 4th Edition

All "Just the Facts101" Material Written or Prepared by Cram101 Publishing

Title Page

Visit Cram101.com for full Practice Exams

WHY STOP HERE... THERE'S MORE ONLINE

With technology and experience, we've developed tools that make studying easier and efficient. Like this Cram101 textbook notebook, Cram101.com offers you the highlights from every chapter of your actual textbook. However, unlike this notebook, **Cram101.com** gives you practice tests for each of the chapters. You also get access to in-depth reference material for writing essays and papers.

By purchasing this book, you get 50% off the normal subscription free!. Just enter the promotional code **'DK73DW21549'** on the Cram101.com registration screen.

CRAM101.COM FEATURES:

Outlines & Highlights
Just like the ones in this notebook, but with links to additional information.

Integrated Note Taking
Add your class notes to the Cram101 notes, print them and maximize your study time.

Problem Solving
Step-by-step walk throughs for math, stats and other disciplines.

Practice Exams
Five different test taking formats for every chapter.

Easy Access
Study any of your books, on any computer, anywhere.

Unlimited Textbooks
All the features above for virtually all your textbooks, just add them to your account at no additional cost.

Be sure to use the promo code above when registering on Cram101.com to get 50% off your membership fees.

Visit Cram101.com for full Practice Exams

STUDYING MADE EASY

This Cram101 notebook is designed to make studying easier and increase your comprehension of the textbook material. Instead of starting with a blank notebook and trying to write down everything discussed in class lectures, you can use this Cram101 textbook notebook and annotate your notes along with the lecture.

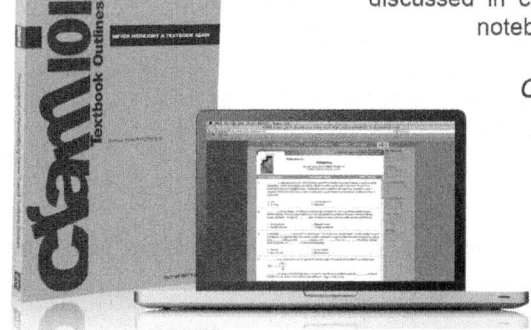

Our goal is to give you the best tools for success.

For a supreme understanding of the course, pair your notebook with our online tools. Should you decide you prefer Cram101.com as your study tool,

we'd like to offer you a trade...

Our Trade In program is a simple way for us to keep our promise and provide you the best studying tools, regardless of where you purchased your Cram101 textbook notebook. As long as your notebook is in *Like New Condition**, you can send it back to us and we will immediately give you a Cram101.com account free for 120 days!

Let The *Trade In* Begin!

THREE SIMPLE STEPS TO TRADE:

1. Go to www.cram101.com/tradein and fill out the packing slip information.
2. Submit and print the packing slip and mail it in with your Cram101 textbook notebook.
3. Activate your account after you receive your email confirmation.

* Books must be returned in *Like New Condition*, meaning there is no damage to the book including, but not limited to; ripped or torn pages, markings or writing on pages, or folded / creased pages. Upon receiving the book, Cram101 will inspect it and reserves the right to terminate your free Cram101.com account and return your textbook notebook at the owners expense.

Visit Cram101.com for full Practice Exams

cram101
LEARNING SYSTEM

"Just the Facts101" is a Cram101 publication and tool designed to give you all the facts from your textbooks. Visit Cram101.com for the full practice test for each of your chapters for virtually any of your textbooks.

Cram101 has built custom study tools specific to your textbook. We provide all of the factual testable information and unlike traditional study guides, we will never send you back to your textbook for more information.

YOU WILL NEVER HAVE TO HIGHLIGHT A BOOK AGAIN!

Cram101 StudyGuides
All of the information in this StudyGuide is written specifically for your textbook. We include the key terms, places, people, and concepts... the information you can expect on your next exam!

Want to take a practice test?
Throughout each chapter of this StudyGuide you will find links to cram101.com where you can select specific chapters to take a complete test on, or you can subscribe and get practice tests for up to 12 of your textbooks, along with other exclusive cram101.com tools like problem solving labs and reference libraries.

Cram101.com
Only cram101.com gives you the outlines, highlights, and PRACTICE TESTS specific to your textbook. Cram101.com is an online application where you'll discover study tools designed to make the most of your limited study time.

By purchasing this book, you get 50% off the normal monthly subscription fee!. Just enter the promotional code **'DK73DW21549'** on the Cram101.com registration screen.

www.Cram101.com

Copyright © 2013 by Cram101, Inc. All rights reserved.
"Just the FACTS101"®, "Cram101"® and "Never Highlight a Book Again!"® are registered trademarks of Cram101, Inc.
ISBN(s): 9781478454557. PUBE-8.201342

Learning System

facts101

Essentials of Sociology
Anthony Giddens, 4th

CONTENTS

1. Sociology: Theory and Method 5
2. Culture and Society 20
3. Socialization, the Life Course, and Aging 31
4. Social Interaction and Everyday Life in the Age of the Internet 41
5. Groups, Networks, and Organizations 50
6. conformity, Deviance, and Crime 63
7. Stratification, Class, and Inequality 76
8. Global Inequality 90
9. Gender Inequality 101
10. Ethnicity and Race 110
11. Families and Intimate Relationships 122
12. Education and Religion 129
13. Politics and Economic Life 137
14. The Sociology of the Body: Health, Illness, and Sexuality 150
15. Urbanization, Population, and the Environment 160
16. Globalization in a Changing World 173

Visit Cram101.com for full Practice Exams

Chapter 1. Sociology: Theory and Method

CHAPTER OUTLINE: KEY TERMS, PEOPLE, PLACES, CONCEPTS

_____ Emile Durkheim

_____ Bullying

_____ Cyberbullying

_____ Suicide

_____ Karl Marx

_____ Sociological imagination

_____ Taliban

_____ Cocaine

_____ Social stratification

_____ Social change

_____ Anomie

_____ Organic solidarity

_____ Social fact

_____ Max Weber

_____ Capitalism

_____ Harriet Martineau

_____ George Herbert Mead

_____ William Julius Wilson

_____ Kwame Nkrumah

Visit Cram101.com for full Practice Exams

Chapter 1. Sociology: Theory and Method
CHAPTER OUTLINE: KEY TERMS, PEOPLE, PLACES, CONCEPTS

- _____ Double consciousness
- _____ Symbolic interactionism
- _____ Functionalism
- _____ Manifest and latent functions
- _____ Self-consciousness
- _____ Marxism
- _____ Femininity
- _____ Postmodernism
- _____ Jean Baudrillard
- _____ Macrosociology
- _____ Microsociology
- _____ Ethnography
- _____ Participant observation
- _____ Sampling
- _____ Random sampling
- _____ Tearoom Trade
- _____ Ethical dilemma
- _____ Human sexuality
- _____ Triangulation

Visit Cram101.com for full Practice Exams

Chapter 1. Sociology: Theory and Method

CHAPTER OUTLINE: KEY TERMS, PEOPLE, PLACES, CONCEPTS

	Debriefing
	Informed consent

CHAPTER HIGHLIGHTS & NOTES: KEY TERMS, PEOPLE, PLACES, CONCEPTS

Emile Durkheim	David Emile Durkheim (April 15, 1858 - November 15, 1917) was a French sociologist. One of his primary goals was to establish sociology as a recognized academic discipline, a goal in which he succeeded. He formally established it as an academic discipline and, with Karl Marx and Max Weber, is commonly cited as the principal architect of modern social science and father of sociology.
Bullying	Bullying is a form of abuse. It involves repeated acts over time attempting to create or enforce one person's (or group's) power over another person (or group), thus an 'imbalance of power'. The 'imbalance of power' may be social power and/or physical power.
Cyberbullying	Cyberbullying is the use of the Internet and related technologies to harm other people, in a deliberate, repeated, and hostile manner. As it has become more common in society, particularly among young people, legislation and awareness campaigns have arisen to combat it. The term 'cyberbullying' was first coined and defined by Canadian educator and anti-bullying activist Bill Belsey, as 'the use of information and communication technologies to support deliberate, repeated, and hostile behavior by an individual or group, that is intended to harm others.' Cyberbullying has subsequently been defined as 'when the Internet, cell phones or other devices are used to send or post text or images intended to hurt or embarrass another person'.
Suicide	Suicide was one of the groundbreaking books in the field of sociology. Written by French sociologist Émile Durkheim and published in 1897 it was a case study (some argue that it is not a case study, and that this is what makes it unique among other scholarly work on the same subject) of suicide, a publication unique for its time which provided an example of what the sociological monograph should look like.

Visit Cram101.com for full Practice Exams

Chapter 1. Sociology: Theory and Method

CHAPTER HIGHLIGHTS & NOTES: KEY TERMS, PEOPLE, PLACES, CONCEPTS

Karl Marx | Karl Heinrich Marx (5 May 1818 - 14 March 1883) was a German philosopher, economist, sociologist, historian, journalist, and revolutionary socialist. His ideas played a significant role in the development of social science and the socialist political movement. He published various books during his lifetime, with the most notable being The Communist Manifesto (1848) and Capital (1867-1894); some of his works were co-written with his friend, the fellow German revolutionary socialist Friedrich Engels.

Born into a wealthy middle class family in Trier, formerly in Prussian Rhineland now called Rhineland-Palatinate, Marx studied at both the University of Bonn and the University of Berlin, where he became interested in the philosophical ideas of the Young Hegelians. In 1836, he became engaged to Jenny von Westphalen, marrying her in 1843. After his studies, he wrote for a radical newspaper in Cologne, and began to work out his theory of dialectical materialism. Moving to Paris in 1843, he began writing for other radical newspapers. He met Engels in Paris, and the two men worked together on a series of books. Exiled to Brussels, he became a leading figure of the Communist League, before moving back to Cologne, where he founded his own newspaper. In 1849 he was exiled again and moved to London together with his wife and children. In London, where the family was reduced to poverty, Marx continued writing and formulating his theories about the nature of society and how he believed it could be improved, as well as campaigning for socialism and becoming a significant figure in the International Workingmen's Association.

Marx's theories about society, economics and politics, which are collectively known as Marxism, hold that all societies progress through the dialectic of class struggle; a conflict between an ownership class which controls production and a lower class which produces the labour for such goods. Heavily critical of the current socio-economic form of society, capitalism, he called it the 'dictatorship of the bourgeoisie', believing it to be run by the wealthy classes purely for their own benefit, and predicted that, like previous socioeconomic systems, it would inevitably produce internal tensions which would lead to its self-destruction and replacement by a new system, socialism. He argued that under socialism society would be governed by the working class in what he called the 'dictatorship of the proletariat', the 'workers state' or 'workers' democracy'. He believed that socialism would, in its turn, eventually be replaced by a stateless, classless society called communism. Along with believing in the inevitability of socialism and communism, Marx actively fought for the former's implementation, arguing that both social theorists and underprivileged people should carry out organised revolutionary action to topple capitalism and bring about socio-economic change.

Revolutionary socialist governments espousing Marxist concepts took power in a variety of countries in the 20th century, leading to the formation of such socialist states as the Soviet Union in 1922 and the People's Republic of China in 1949, while various theoretical variants, such as Leninism, Stalinism, Trotskyism and Maoism, were developed. Marx is typically cited, with Émile Durkheim and Max Weber, as one of the three principal architects of modern social science.

Chapter 1. Sociology: Theory and Method

CHAPTER HIGHLIGHTS & NOTES: KEY TERMS, PEOPLE, PLACES, CONCEPTS

Marx has been described as one of the most influential figures in human history, and in a 1999 BBC poll was voted the top 'thinker of the millennium' by people from around the world. Biography Early life: 1818-1835

Karl Heinrich Marx was born on 5 May 1818 at 664 Brückergasse in Trier, a town located in the Kingdom of Prussia's Province of the Lower Rhine. His ancestry was Jewish, with his paternal line having supplied the rabbis of Trier since 1723, a role that had been taken up by his own grandfather, Meier Halevi Marx; Meier's son and Karl's father would be the first in the line to receive a secular education. His maternal grandfather was a Dutch rabbi. Karl's father, Herschel Marx, was middle-class and relatively wealthy: the family owned a number of Moselle vineyards; he converted from Judaism to the Protestant Christian denomination of Lutheranism prior to his son's birth, taking on the German forename of Heinrich over Herschel. In 1815, he began working as an attorney and in 1819 moved his family from a five-room rented apartment into a ten-room property near the Porta Nigra. A man of the Enlightenment, Heinrich Marx was interested in the ideas of the philosophers Immanuel Kant and Voltaire, and took part in agitation for a constitution and reforms in Prussia, which was then governed by an absolute monarchy. Karl's mother, born Henrietta Pressburg, was a Dutch Jew who, unlike her husband, was only semi-literate. She claimed to suffer from 'excessive mother love', devoting much time to her family, and insisting on cleanliness within her home. She was from a prosperous business family. Her family later founded the company Philips Electronics: she was great-aunt to Anton and Gerard Philips, and great-great-aunt to Frits Philips. Her brother, Marx's uncle Benjamin Philips (1830-1900), was a wealthy banker and industrialist, who Karl and Jenny Marx would later often come rely upon for loans, while they were exiled in London.

Little is known about Karl Marx's childhood.

Sociological imagination

The term sociological imagination was coined by the American sociologist C. Wright Mills in 1959, to describe the type of insight offered by the discipline of sociology. The term is used in introductory textbooks in sociology to explain the nature of sociology and its relevance in daily life.

Sociologists differ in their understanding of the concept, but the range suggests several important commonalities.

Taliban

The Taliban, alternative spelling Taleban, is an Islamist militia group that ruled large parts of Afghanistan from September 1996 onwards. Although in control of Afghanistan's capital (Kabul) and most of the country for five years, the Taliban's Islamic Emirate of Afghanistan gained diplomatic recognition from only three states: Pakistan, Saudi Arabia, and the United Arab Emirates. After the attacks of September 11 2001 the Taliban regime was overthrown by Operation Enduring Freedom.

Chapter 1. Sociology: Theory and Method

CHAPTER HIGHLIGHTS & NOTES: KEY TERMS, PEOPLE, PLACES, CONCEPTS

Cocaine	Cocaine is a 1922 British crime film directed by Graham Cutts and starring Hilda Bayley, Flora Le Breton, Ward McAllister and Cyril Raymond. A melodrama - it depicts the distribution of cocaine by gangsters through a series of London nightclubs and the revenge sought by a man after the death of his daughter. Because of its depiction of drug use, it was the most controversial British film of the 1920s.
Social stratification	In sociology, social stratification is a concept involving the 'classification of persons into groups based on shared socio-economic conditions ... a relational set of inequalities with economic, social, political and ideological dimensions.' It is a system by which society ranks categories of people in a hierarchy Social stratification is based on four basic principles: (1) Social stratification is a trait of society, not simply a reflection of individual differences; (2) Social stratification carries over from generation to generation; (3) Social stratification is universal but variable; (4) Social stratification involves not just inequality but beliefs as well. In modern Western societies, stratification is broadly organized into three main layers: upper class, middle class, and lower class. Each of these classes can be further subdivided into smaller classes (e.g. occupational).
Social change	Social change refers to an alteration in the social order of a society. It may refer to the notion of social progress or sociocultural evolution, the philosophical idea that society moves forward by dialectical or evolutionary means. It may refer to a paradigmatic change in the socio-economic structure, for instance a shift away from feudalism and towards capitalism.
Anomie	Anomie is a sociological term meaning 'personal feeling of a lack of social norms; normlessness'. It describes the breakdown of social norms and values. It was popularized by French sociologist Émile Durkheim in his influential book Suicide (1897).
Organic solidarity	Organic solidarity comes from the interdependence that arises from specialization of work and the complementarities between people--a development which occurs in 'modern' and 'industrial' societies. Definition: it is social cohesion based upon the dependence individuals have on each other in more advanced societies. Although individuals perform different tasks and often have different values and interest, the order and very solidarity of society depends on their reliance on each other to perform their specified tasks. Organic here is referring to the interdependence of the component parts.
Social fact	In sociology, social facts those phenomena arising only in the creative association of individuals. They are the values, cultural norms, and social structures which transcend the individual and are capable of exercising a social constraint.

Chapter 1. Sociology: Theory and Method

CHAPTER HIGHLIGHTS & NOTES: KEY TERMS, PEOPLE, PLACES, CONCEPTS

Max Weber	Karl Emil Maximilian 'Max' Weber was a German sociologist and political economist who profoundly influenced social theory, social research, and the discipline of sociology itself.
	Weber was a key proponent of methodological antipositivism, presenting sociology as a non-empiricist field which must study social action through interpretive means based upon understanding the meanings and purposes that individuals attach to their own actions. Weber is often cited, with Émile Durkheim and Karl Marx, as one of the three principal architects of modern social science.
	Weber's main intellectual concern was understanding the processes of rationalisation, secularization, and 'disenchantment' that he associated with the rise of capitalism and modernity. Weber is perhaps best known for his thesis combining economic sociology and the sociology of religion, elaborated in his book The Protestant Ethic and the Spirit of Capitalism. Weber proposed that ascetic Protestantism was one of the major 'elective affinities' associated with the rise of capitalism, bureaucracy and the rational-legal nation-state in the Western world. Against Marx's 'historical materialism,' Weber emphasised the importance of cultural influences embedded in religion as a means for understanding the genesis of capitalism. The Protestant Ethic formed the earliest part in Weber's broader investigations into world religion: he would go on to examine the religions of China, the religions of India and ancient Judaism, with particular regard to the apparent non-development of capitalism in the corresponding societies, as well as to their differing forms of social stratification.
	In another major work, Politics as a Vocation, Weber defined the state as an entity which successfully claims a 'monopoly on the legitimate use of violence'. He was also the first to categorize social authority into distinct forms, which he labelled as charismatic, traditional, and rational-legal. His analysis of bureaucracy emphasised that modern state institutions are increasingly based on rational-legal authority. Weber also made a variety of other contributions in economic history, as well as economic theory and methodology. Weber's thought on modernity and rationalisation would come to facilitate critical theory of the Frankfurt school.
	After the First World War, Max Weber was among the founders of the liberal German Democratic Party.
Capitalism	Capitalism is generally considered to be an economic system that is based on the legal ability to make a return on capital. Some have also used the term as a synonym for competitive markets, wage labor, capital accumulation, voluntary exchange, personal finance and greed. The designation is applied to a variety of historical cases, varying in time, geography, politics, and culture.
Harriet Martineau	Harriet Martineau was an English social theorist and Whig writer, often cited as the first female sociologist.

Chapter 1. Sociology: Theory and Method

CHAPTER HIGHLIGHTS & NOTES: KEY TERMS, PEOPLE, PLACES, CONCEPTS

	Martineau wrote 35 books and a multitude of essays from a sociological, holistic, religious, domestic, and, perhaps most controversial, a feminine perspective; she also translated various works from Auguste Comte. She earned enough to be supported entirely by her writing, a challenging feat for a woman in the Victorian era.
George Herbert Mead	George Herbert Mead was an American philosopher, sociologist and psychologist, primarily affiliated with the University of Chicago, where he was one of several distinguished pragmatists. He is regarded as one of the founders of social psychology and the American sociological tradition in general.
	Mead was born February 27, 1863 in South Hadley, Massachusetts.
William Julius Wilson	William Julius Wilson is an American sociologist. He worked at the University of Chicago 1972-1996 before moving to Harvard.
	William Julius Wilson is Lewis P. and Linda L. Geyser University Professor at Harvard University.
Kwame Nkrumah	The Rt. Hon. Dr. Kwame Nkrumah P.C., was the leader of Ghana and its predecessor state, the Gold Coast, from 1951 to 1966. Overseeing the nation's independence from British colonial rule in 1957, Nkrumah was the first President of Ghana and the first Prime Minister of Ghana.
Double consciousness	Double consciousness is a term coined by W. E. B. Du Bois. The term is used to describe an individual whose identity is divided into several facets. Du Bois saw double consciousness as a useful theoretical model for understanding the psycho-social divisions existing in the American society.
Symbolic interactionism	Symbolic Interaction, or the ongoing use of language and gestures in anticipation of how the other will react; a conversation. Symbolic interactionism isn't just talk. Both the verbal and nonverbal responses that a listener then delivers are similarly constructed in expectation of how the original speaker will react. The ongoing process is like the game of charades; only it's a full-fledged conversation.
Functionalism	Functionalism is a theory of the mind in contemporary philosophy, developed largely as an alternative to both the identity theory of mind and behaviourism. Its core idea is that mental states (beliefs, desires, being in pain, etc). are constituted solely by their functional role -- that is, they are causal relations to other mental states, sensory inputs, and behavioral outputs.
Manifest and latent functions	Manifest and latent functions are social scientific concepts first clarified for sociology by Robert K. Merton. Merton appeared interested in sharpening the conceptual tools to be employed in a functional analysis.

Chapter 1. Sociology: Theory and Method

CHAPTER HIGHLIGHTS & NOTES: KEY TERMS, PEOPLE, PLACES, CONCEPTS

	Manifest functions and dysfunctions are conscious and deliberate, the latent ones the unconscious and unintended. While functions are intended (manifest) or recognized (latent), and have a positive effect on society, dysfunctions are unintended (manifest) or unrecognized (latent) and have a negative effect on society.
Self-consciousness	Self-consciousness is an acute sense of self-awareness. It is a preoccupation with oneself, as opposed to the philosophical state of self-awareness, which is the awareness that one exists as an individual being; although some writers use both terms interchangeably or synonymously. An unpleasant feeling of self-consciousness may occur when one realizes that one is being watched or observed, the feeling that 'everyone is looking' at oneself.
Marxism	Marxism is an economic and socio-political worldview that contains within it a political ideology for how to change and improve society by implementing socialism. Originally developed in the early to mid 19th century by two German émigrés living in Britain, Karl Marx and Friedrich Engels, Marxism is based upon a materialist interpretation of history. Taking the idea that social change occurs because of the struggle between different classes within society who are under contradiction one against the other, the Marxist analysis leads to the conclusion that capitalism, the currently dominant form of economic management, leads to the oppression of the proletariat, who not only make up the majority of the world's populace but who also spend their lives working for the benefit of the bourgeoisie, or the wealthy ruling class in society.
Femininity	Femininity is the set of female qualities attributed specifically to women and girls by a particular culture. The complement to femininity is masculinity. Feminine attributes These are often associated with life-giving and nurturing qualities of elegance, gentleness, motherhood, birth, intuition, creativity, life-death-rebirth and biological life cycle.
Postmodernism	Postmodernism is a range of conceptual frameworks and ideologies that are defined in opposition to those commonly associated with ideologies of modernity and modernist notions of knowledge and science, such as formalism, materialism, metaphysics, positivism, realism, reductionism, and structuralism. Postmodernism is not a philosophical movement, but rather a number of philosophical and critical methods. In other words, postmodernism is not a method of doing philosophy, but rather a way of approaching traditional ideas and practices in non-traditional ways that deviate from pre-established superstructural modes.
Jean Baudrillard	Jean Baudrillard was a French sociologist, philosopher, cultural theorist, political commentator, and photographer. His work is frequently associated with postmodernism and specifically post-structuralism.

Visit Cram101.com for full Practice Exams

Chapter 1. Sociology: Theory and Method

CHAPTER HIGHLIGHTS & NOTES: KEY TERMS, PEOPLE, PLACES, CONCEPTS

	Baudrillard was born in Reims, northeastern France, on July 27, 1929. He told interviewers that his grandparents were peasants and his parents were civil servants.
Macrosociology	Macrosociology is an approach to the discipline which emphasizes the analysis of social systems and populations on a large scale, at the level of social structure, and often at a necessarily high level of theoretical abstraction. Microsociology, by contrast, focuses on the individual social agency. Macrosociology also concerns individuals, families, and other constituent aspects of a society, but always does so in relation to larger social system of which they are a part.
Microsociology	Microsociology is one of the main branches of sociology, concerning the nature of everyday human social interactions and agency on a small scale: face to face. Microsociology is based on interpretative analysis rather than statistical or empirical observation, and shares close association with the philosophy of phenomenology. Methods includes symbolic interactionism and ethnomethodology; ethnomethodology in particular has led to many academic sub-divisions and studies such as microlinguistical research and other related aspects of human social behaviour.
Ethnography	Ethnography is a qualitative research method aimed to learn and understand cultural phenomena which reflect the knowledge and system of meanings guiding the life of a cultural group. It was pioneered in the field of socio-cultural anthropology but has also become a popular method in various other fields of social sciences--particularly in sociology, communication studies, and history --that study people, ethnic groups and other ethnic formations, their ethnogenesis, composition, resettlement, social welfare characteristics, as well as their material and spiritual culture. It is often employed for gathering empirical data on human societies and cultures.
Participant observation	Participant observation is a structured type of research strategy. It is a widely used methodology in many disciplines, particularly, cultural anthropology, but also sociology, communication studies, and social psychology. Its aim is to gain a close and intimate familiarity with a given group of individuals (such as a religious, occupational, or sub cultural group, or a particular community) and their practices through an intensive involvement with people in their cultural environment, usually over an extended period of time.
Sampling	In statistics and survey methodology, sampling is concerned with the selection of a subset of individuals from within a population to estimate characteristics of the whole population.
	Researchers rarely survey the entire population because the cost of a census is too high.

Visit Cram101.com for full Practice Exams

Chapter 1. Sociology: Theory and Method

CHAPTER HIGHLIGHTS & NOTES: KEY TERMS, PEOPLE, PLACES, CONCEPTS

Random sampling	In random sampling every combination of items from the frame, or stratum, has a known probability of occurring, but these probabilities are not necessarily equal. With any form of sampling there is a risk that the sample may not adequately represent the population but with random sampling there is a large body of statistical theory which quantifies the risk and thus enables an appropriate sample size to be chosen.
Tearoom Trade	Tearoom Trade is a title of a controversial 1970 Ph.D. dissertation and book 'Tearoom trade: a study of homosexual encounters in public places' by Laud Humphreys. The study is an analysis of homosexual acts taking place in public toilets. Humphreys asserted that the men participating in such activity came from diverse social backgrounds, had differing personal motives for seeking homosexual contact in such venues, and variously self-perceived as 'straight,' 'bisexual,' or 'gay.' His study called into question some of the stereotypes associated with the anonymous male-male sexual encounters in public places, demonstrating that many of the participants lived otherwise conventional lives as family men and respected members of their communities, and that their activities posed no danger of harassment to straight males.
Ethical dilemma	Ethical dilemma is a complex situation that will often involve an apparent mental conflict between moral imperatives, in which to obey one would result in transgressing another. This is also called an ethical paradox since in moral philosophy, paradox often plays a central role in ethics debates. 'Love your neighbour' (Gospel of Matthew 5:43) is sometimes in contradiction to an armed rapist: if he succeeds, you will not be able to love him.
Human sexuality	Human sexuality is how people experience the erotic and express themselves as sexual beings; the awareness of themselves as males or females; the capacity they have for erotic experiences and responses. Human sexuality can be described as the way someone is attracted another person of the opposite sex (heterosexuality), to the same sex (homosexuality), or attracted to both sexes (bisexuality).
	It used to be believed that human sexual behavior was different from the sexual behavior of most other animals, in that it was practiced for reasons besides copulation.
Triangulation	Triangulation is most commonly used to express a situation in which one family member will not communicate directly with another family member, but will communicate with a third family member, which can lead to the third family member becoming part of the triangle. The concept originated in the study of dysfunctional family systems, but can describe behaviors in other systems as well, including work.
	Triangulation can also be used as a label for a form of 'splitting' in which one person plays the third family member against one that he or she is upset about.
Debriefing	Debriefing is a process of questioning to gain information from an individual.

Chapter 1. Sociology: Theory and Method

CHAPTER HIGHLIGHTS & NOTES: KEY TERMS, PEOPLE, PLACES, CONCEPTS

	Debriefings are used by grief counselors and disaster workers as part of an emergency intervention to help people who have recently experienced major loss or suffering. These cases include hurricanes, earthquakes, school shootings, and other situations that involve fear, injury, extreme discomfort, property damage, or loss of friends and loved ones.
Informed consent	Informed consent is a phrase often used in law to indicate that the consent a person gives meets certain minimum standards. As a literal matter, in the absence of fraud, it is redundant. An informed consent can be said to have been given based upon a clear appreciation and understanding of the facts, implications, and future consequences of an action.

CHAPTER QUIZ: KEY TERMS, PEOPLE, PLACES, CONCEPTS

1. _____ is a range of conceptual frameworks and ideologies that are defined in opposition to those commonly associated with ideologies of modernity and modernist notions of knowledge and science, such as formalism, materialism, metaphysics, positivism, realism, reductionism, and structuralism. _____ is not a philosophical movement, but rather a number of philosophical and critical methods. In other words, _____ is not a method of doing philosophy, but rather a way of approaching traditional ideas and practices in non-traditional ways that deviate from pre-established superstructural modes.

    a. Neomodern
    b. Postmodernism
    c. Contemporary art
    d. Critical historiography

2. In statistics and survey methodology, _____ is concerned with the selection of a subset of individuals from within a population to estimate characteristics of the whole population.

    Researchers rarely survey the entire population because the cost of a census is too high. The three main advantages of _____ are that the cost is lower, data collection is faster, and since the data set is smaller it is possible to ensure homogeneity and to improve the accuracy and quality of the data.

    a. Scale analysis
    b. Structured concept mapping
    c. Sampling
    d. Survey Methodology

3. . _____ is the set of female qualities attributed specifically to women and girls by a particular culture.

Visit Cram101.com for full Practice Exams

Chapter 1. Sociology: Theory and Method

CHAPTER QUIZ: KEY TERMS, PEOPLE, PLACES, CONCEPTS

The complement to _____ is masculinity.

Feminine attributes

These are often associated with life-giving and nurturing qualities of elegance, gentleness, motherhood, birth, intuition, creativity, life-death-rebirth and biological life cycle.

a. Gender and suicide
b. Gender binary
c. Gender continuum
d. Femininity

4. _____ is one of the main branches of sociology, concerning the nature of everyday human social interactions and agency on a small scale: face to face. _____ is based on interpretative analysis rather than statistical or empirical observation, and shares close association with the philosophy of phenomenology. Methods includes symbolic interactionism and ethnomethodology; ethnomethodology in particular has led to many academic sub-divisions and studies such as microlinguistical research and other related aspects of human social behaviour.

a. Political sociology
b. Sociology of punishment
c. Sociology of scientific knowledge
d. Microsociology

5. The _____, alternative spelling Taleban, is an Islamist militia group that ruled large parts of Afghanistan from September 1996 onwards. Although in control of Afghanistan's capital (Kabul) and most of the country for five years, the _____'s Islamic Emirate of Afghanistan gained diplomatic recognition from only three states: Pakistan, Saudi Arabia, and the United Arab Emirates. After the attacks of September 11 2001 the _____ regime was overthrown by Operation Enduring Freedom.

a. Terrorism
b. Thai gem scam
c. Thai tailor scam
d. Taliban

Visit Cram101.com for full Practice Exams

ANSWER KEY
Chapter 1. Sociology: Theory and Method

1. b
2. c
3. d
4. d
5. d

You can take the complete Chapter Practice Test

for Chapter 1. Sociology: Theory and Method
on all key terms, persons, places, and concepts.

Online 99 Cents

http://www.epub4.5.21549.1.cram101.com/

Use www.Cram101.com for all your study needs

including Cram101's online interactive problem solving labs in

chemistry, statistics, mathematics, and more.

Chapter 2. Culture and Society

CHAPTER OUTLINE: KEY TERMS, PEOPLE, PLACES, CONCEPTS

- Emile Durkheim
- Eye contact
- Norm
- Instinct
- Inuit
- Conformity
- Social control
- Sociobiology
- Cultural diversity
- Assimilation
- Counterculture
- Cultural group
- Cultural identity
- Ethnocentrism
- Multiculturalism
- Clitoridectomy
- Cultural universal
- Incarceration
- Material culture

Visit Cram101.com for full Practice Exams

Chapter 2. Culture and Society

CHAPTER OUTLINE: KEY TERMS, PEOPLE, PLACES, CONCEPTS

	Semiotics
	Agrarian society
	Pastoral society
	Civilization
	Colonialism
	International development
	Globalization
	Popular culture
	Arab Spring
	Taliban

CHAPTER HIGHLIGHTS & NOTES: KEY TERMS, PEOPLE, PLACES, CONCEPTS

Emile Durkheim	David Emile Durkheim (April 15, 1858 - November 15, 1917) was a French sociologist. One of his primary goals was to establish sociology as a recognized academic discipline, a goal in which he succeeded. He formally established it as an academic discipline and, with Karl Marx and Max Weber, is commonly cited as the principal architect of modern social science and father of sociology.
Eye contact	Eye contact is a meeting of the eyes between two individuals. In human beings, eye contact is a form of nonverbal communication and is thought to have a large influence on social behavior.

Visit Cram101.com for full Practice Exams

Chapter 2. Culture and Society

CHAPTER HIGHLIGHTS & NOTES: KEY TERMS, PEOPLE, PLACES, CONCEPTS

Norm | Social norms are the behaviors and cues within a society or group. This sociological term has been defined as 'the rules that a group uses for appropriate and inappropriate values, beliefs, attitudes and behaviors. These rules may be explicit or implicit.

Instinct | Instinct is a two-part drama serial which premièred on ITV (ITV1STVUTV) on 26 February 2007. It was created and written by Lizzie Mickery, and produced by Tightrope Pictures for ITV. The serial follows Detective Chief Inspector Thomas Flynn, played by Anthony Flanagan, as he hunts a serial killer in the Lancashire Pennines, while dealing with a troubled personal life.

Mickery, who had previously written the first three series of the similarly themed Messiah, described Instinct as a character-driven whodunit, which placed the emotional lives of the characters at the forefront of the drama. In creating the lead character of Thomas Flynn, she wanted to explore 'why sometimes somebody who is a good detective is fallible as a man.' Flynn is a thirtysomething, contemporary character who is not 'the usual middle-aged detective, disillusioned and world weary with a broken marriage and a love of scotch.' Flynn's defining characteristics are that he relishes his work, is emotionally detached and has acute powers of observation.

Inuit | The Inuit are a group of culturally similar indigenous peoples inhabiting the Arctic regions of Canada (Northwest Territories, Nunatsiavut, Nunavik, Nunavut, Nunatukavut), Denmark (Greenland), Russia (Siberia) and the United States (Alaska). Inuit means 'the people' in the Inuktitut language. An Inuk is an Inuit person.

Conformity | Conformity is the act of matching attitudes, beliefs, and behaviors to group norms. Norms are implicit rules shared by a group of individuals, that guide their interactions with others and among society or social group. This tendency to conform occurs in small groups and/or society as a whole, and may result from subtle unconscious influences, or direct and overt social pressure.

Social control | Social control refers generally to societal and political mechanisms or processes that regulate individual and group behavior, leading to conformity and compliance to the rules of a given society, state, or social group. Many mechanisms of social control are cross-cultural, if only in the control mechanisms used to prevent the establishment of chaos or anomie. Some theorists, such as Émile Durkheim, refer to this form of control as regulation.

Sociobiology | Sociobiology is a field of scientific study which is based on the assumption that social behavior has resulted from evolution and attempts to explain and examine social behavior within that context. Often considered a branch of biology and sociology, it also draws from ethology, anthropology, evolution, zoology, archaeology, population genetics, and other disciplines.

Chapter 2. Culture and Society

CHAPTER HIGHLIGHTS & NOTES: KEY TERMS, PEOPLE, PLACES, CONCEPTS

Cultural diversity	Cultural diversity is the quality of diverse or different cultures, as opposed to monoculture, as in the global monoculture, or a homogenization of cultures, akin to cultural decay. For example, before Hawaii was conquered by Europeans, the culturally diverse Hawaiian culture existed in the world, and contributed to the world's cultural diversity. Now Hawaii has been westernized; the vast majority of its culture has been replaced with Western or American culture.
Assimilation	Cultural assimilation is a socio-political response to demographic multi-ethnicity that supports or promotes the assimilation of ethnic minorities into the dominant culture. It is opposed to affirmative philosophy (for example, multiculturalism) which recognizes and works to maintain differences. The term assimilation is often used with regard to immigrants and various ethnic groups who have settled in a new land.
Counterculture	Counterculture is a sociological term used to describe the values and norms of behavior of a cultural group, or subculture, that run counter to those of the social mainstream of the day, the cultural equivalent of political opposition. It is a neologism attributed to Theodore Roszak. Although distinct countercultural undercurrents have existed in many societies, here the term refers to a more significant, visible phenomenon that reaches critical mass and persists for a period of time.
Cultural group	The nominal term cultural group generally refers to a self-defined group of people who share a commonality of sociological, ethnographic or regional background experiences which identify them as a group. Cultural groups may be defined by many types of commonality, as such, the method of identification supplies the context for the grouping. ==References== A group of people who share common beliefs, value, behavior, these can affect how you relate to other e.g. ethnic (Maori, Pacifier etc), rural urban, youth, beach, sports, religious, hobby etc....
Cultural identity	Cultural identity is the identity of a group or culture, or of an individual as far as one is influenced by one's belonging to a group or culture. Cultural identity is similar to and has overlaps with, but is not synonymous with, identity politics. Various modern cultural studies and social theories have investigated cultural identity.
Ethnocentrism	Ethnocentrism is judging another culture solely by the values and standards of one's own culture. The ethnocentric individual will judge other groups relative to his or her own particular ethnic group or culture, especially with concern to language, behavior, customs, and religion.

Chapter 2. Culture and Society

CHAPTER HIGHLIGHTS & NOTES: KEY TERMS, PEOPLE, PLACES, CONCEPTS

Multiculturalism	Multiculturalism is an ideology that promotes the institutionalisation of communities containing multiple cultures. It is generally applied to the demographic make-up of a specific place, usually at the organizational level, e.g. schools, businesses, neighbourhoods, cities, or nations. In a political context the term is used for a wide variety of meanings, ranging from the advocacy of equal respect to the various cultures in a society, to a policy of promoting the maintenance of cultural diversity, to policies in which people of various ethnic and religious groups are addressed by the authorities as defined by the group they belong to.
Clitoridectomy	Clitoridectomy is the surgical removal of the clitoris. It is rarely needed as a therapeutic medical procedure, such as when cancer has developed in or spread to the clitoris. Most removals of the clitoris occur as female genital mutilation, defined by the World Health Organisation as 'all procedures involving partial or total removal of the external female genitalia or other injury to the female genital organs whether for cultural, religious or other non-therapeutic reasons.'.
Cultural universal	A cultural universal as discussed by Emile Durkheim, George Murdock, Claude Lévi-Strauss, Donald Brown and others, is an element, pattern, trait, or institution that is common to all human cultures worldwide. Taken together, the whole body of cultural universals is known as the human condition. Evolutionary psychologists hold that behaviors or traits that occur universally in all cultures are good candidates for evolutionary adaptations.
Incarceration	Incarceration is the detention of a person in prison, typically as punishment for a crime (custodial sentence). People are most commonly incarcerated upon suspicion or conviction of committing a crime, and different jurisdictions have differing laws governing the function of incarceration within a larger system of justice. Incarceration serves four essential purposes with regard to criminals:•to isolate criminals to prevent them from committing more crimes•to punish criminals for committing crimes•to deter others from committing crimes•to rehabilitate criminals Incarceration rates, when measured by the United Nations, are considered distinct and separate from the imprisonment of political prisoners and others not charged with a specific crime.
Material culture	In the social sciences, material culture is a term, developed in the late 19th and early 20th century, that refers to the relationship between artifacts and social relations. Studying a culture's relationship to materiality is a lens through which social and cultural attitudes can be discussed. It is also a term used by historians, sometimes described under the variant term material history, where it means the study of ancient objects in order to understand how a particular culture was organised and functioned over time.

Visit Cram101.com for full Practice Exams

Chapter 2. Culture and Society

CHAPTER HIGHLIGHTS & NOTES: KEY TERMS, PEOPLE, PLACES, CONCEPTS

Semiotics	Semiotics, is the study of signs and sign processes (semiosis), indication, designation, likeness, analogy, metaphor, symbolism, signification, and communication. Semiotics is closely related to the field of linguistics, which, for its part, studies the structure and meaning of language more specifically. Semiotics is often divided into three branches:•Semantics: Relation between signs and the things to which they refer; their denotata, or meaning•Syntactics: Relations among signs in formal structures•Pragmatics: Relation between signs and the effects they have on the people who use them Semiotics is frequently seen as having important anthropological dimensions; for example, Umberto Eco proposes that every cultural phenomenon can be studied as communication.
Agrarian society	An agrarian society is a society that depends on agriculture as its primary means for support and sustenance. The society acknowledges other means of livelihood and work habits but stresses the importance of agriculture and farming, and was the most common form of socio-economic organization for most of recorded human history. This was the common way for Medieval European countries to gain wealth.
Pastoral society	A pastoral society is a social group of pastoralists, whose way of life is based on pastoralism, and is typically nomadic. Daily life is centered upon the tending of herds or flocks. There is not an explicit form of social organization associated with pastoralism.
Civilization	Civilization is a sometimes controversial term which has been used in several related ways. Primarily, the term has been used to refer to human cultures which are complex in terms of technology, science, politics and division of labour. Such civilizations are generally urbanized.
Colonialism	Colonialism is the establishment, maintenance, acquisition and expansion of colonies in one territory by people from another territory. It is a process whereby the metropole claims sovereignty over the colony, and the social structure, government, and economics of the colony are changed by colonizers from the metropole. Colonialism is a set of unequal relationships between the metropole and the colony and between the colonists and the indigenous population.
International development	International development is a concept that lacks a universally accepted definition, but it is most used in a holistic and multi-disciplinary context of human development -- the development of greater quality of life for humans. It therefore encompasses foreign aid, governance, healthcare, education, poverty reduction, gender equality, disaster preparedness, infrastructure, economics, human rights, environment and issues associated with these. International development is different from simple development in that it is specifically composed of institutions and policies that arose after the Second World War.

Chapter 2. Culture and Society

CHAPTER HIGHLIGHTS & NOTES: KEY TERMS, PEOPLE, PLACES, CONCEPTS

Globalization	Globalization refers to the increasing global relationships of culture, people, and economic activity. It is generally used to refer to economic globalization: the global distribution of the production of goods and services, through reduction of barriers to international trade such as tariffs, export fees, and import quotas and the reduction of restrictions on the movement of capital and on investment. Globalization may contribute to economic growth in developed and developing countries through increased specialization and the principle of comparative advantage.
Popular culture	Popular culture is the totality of ideas, perspectives, attitudes, memes, images and other phenomena that are preferred by an informal consensus within the mainstream of a given culture, especially Western culture of the early to mid 20th century and the emerging global mainstream of the late 20th and early 21st century. Heavily influenced by mass media, this collection of ideas permeates the everyday lives of the society. Popular culture is often viewed as being trivial and dumbed-down in order to find consensual acceptance throughout the mainstream.
Arab Spring	The Arab Spring is a revolutionary wave of demonstrations and protests occurring in the Arab world that began on Friday, 17 December 2010. To date, rulers have been forced from power in Tunisia, Egypt, Libya, and Yemen; civil uprisings have erupted in Bahrain and Syria; major protests have broken out in Algeria, Iraq, Jordan, Kuwait, and Morocco; and minor protests have occurred in Lebanon, Mauritania, Oman, Saudi Arabia, Sudan, and Western Sahara. Clashes at the borders of Israel in May 2011, as well as protests by the Arab minority in Iranian Khuzestan and a rebellion in Mali have also been inspired by the regional Arab Spring, while the Malian coup d'état has been described as 'fallout'. The protests have shared techniques of mostly civil resistance in sustained campaigns involving strikes, demonstrations, marches, and rallies, as well as the use of social media to organize, communicate, and raise awareness in the face of state attempts at repression and Internet censorship.
Taliban	The Taliban, alternative spelling Taleban, is an Islamist militia group that ruled large parts of Afghanistan from September 1996 onwards. Although in control of Afghanistan's capital (Kabul) and most of the country for five years, the Taliban's Islamic Emirate of Afghanistan gained diplomatic recognition from only three states: Pakistan, Saudi Arabia, and the United Arab Emirates. After the attacks of September 11 2001 the Taliban regime was overthrown by Operation Enduring Freedom.

Chapter 2. Culture and Society

CHAPTER QUIZ: KEY TERMS, PEOPLE, PLACES, CONCEPTS

1. _____ refers generally to societal and political mechanisms or processes that regulate individual and group behavior, leading to conformity and compliance to the rules of a given society, state, or social group. Many mechanisms of _____ are cross-cultural, if only in the control mechanisms used to prevent the establishment of chaos or anomie. Some theorists, such as Émile Durkheim, refer to this form of control as regulation.

   a. Sousveillance
   b. Spatial reconnaissance
   c. Social control
   d. Surveillance art

2. _____ is the act of matching attitudes, beliefs, and behaviors to group norms. Norms are implicit rules shared by a group of individuals, that guide their interactions with others and among society or social group. This tendency to conform occurs in small groups and/or society as a whole, and may result from subtle unconscious influences, or direct and overt social pressure.

   a. Consensus-seeking decision-making
   b. Cronyism
   c. Conformity
   d. Design by committee

3. _____ is the quality of diverse or different cultures, as opposed to monoculture, as in the global monoculture, or a homogenization of cultures, akin to cultural decay. For example, before Hawaii was conquered by Europeans, the culturally diverse Hawaiian culture existed in the world, and contributed to the world's _____. Now Hawaii has been westernized; the vast majority of its culture has been replaced with Western or American culture.

   a. Cultural subsidy
   b. Culture speculation
   c. Cultural diversity
   d. New Music Economy

4. The _____ are a group of culturally similar indigenous peoples inhabiting the Arctic regions of Canada (Northwest Territories, Nunatsiavut, Nunavik, Nunavut, Nunatukavut), Denmark (Greenland), Russia (Siberia) and the United States (Alaska). _____ means 'the people' in the Inuktitut language. An Inuk is an _____ person.

   a. Kalaallit
   b. Koryaks
   c. Sadlermiut
   d. Inuit

5. . _____ is the totality of ideas, perspectives, attitudes, memes, images and other phenomena that are preferred by an informal consensus within the mainstream of a given culture, especially Western culture of the early to mid 20th century and the emerging global mainstream of the late 20th and early 21st century. Heavily influenced by mass media, this collection of ideas permeates the everyday lives of the society.

Visit Cram101.com for full Practice Exams

Chapter 2. Culture and Society

CHAPTER QUIZ: KEY TERMS, PEOPLE, PLACES, CONCEPTS

_____ is often viewed as being trivial and dumbed-down in order to find consensual acceptance throughout the mainstream.

a. Positive youth development
b. Preadolescence
c. Ragging
d. Popular culture

Visit Cram101.com for full Practice Exams

ANSWER KEY
Chapter 2. Culture and Society

1. c
2. c
3. c
4. d
5. d

You can take the complete Chapter Practice Test

for Chapter 2. Culture and Society
on all key terms, persons, places, and concepts.

Online 99 Cents

http://www.epub4.5.21549.2.cram101.com/

Use www.Cram101.com for all your study needs

including Cram101's online interactive problem solving labs in

chemistry, statistics, mathematics, and more.

Chapter 3. Socialization, the Life Course, and Aging

CHAPTER OUTLINE: KEY TERMS, PEOPLE, PLACES, CONCEPTS

- _____ Social reproduction
- _____ George Herbert Mead
- _____ Cognition
- _____ Self-consciousness
- _____ Jean Piaget
- _____ Egocentrism
- _____ Generalized other
- _____ Agent
- _____ Mass media
- _____ Tron
- _____ Arranged marriage
- _____ Identity
- _____ Childhood
- _____ Functionalism
- _____ Activity theory
- _____ Social class
- _____ Social conflict
- _____ Baby boomer
- _____ Medicare

Visit Cram101.com for full Practice Exams

Chapter 3. Socialization, the Life Course, and Aging
CHAPTER OUTLINE: KEY TERMS, PEOPLE, PLACES, CONCEPTS

	Social security
	Health insurance
	Elder abuse
	Nursing home
	Social isolation
	Ageism

CHAPTER HIGHLIGHTS & NOTES: KEY TERMS, PEOPLE, PLACES, CONCEPTS

Social reproduction	Social reproduction is a sociological term referring to processes which sustain or perpetuate characteristics of a given social structure or tradition over a period of time.
George Herbert Mead	George Herbert Mead was an American philosopher, sociologist and psychologist, primarily affiliated with the University of Chicago, where he was one of several distinguished pragmatists. He is regarded as one of the founders of social psychology and the American sociological tradition in general.
	Mead was born February 27, 1863 in South Hadley, Massachusetts.
Cognition	In science, cognition is a group of mental processes that includes attention, memory, producing and understanding language, learning, reasoning, problem solving, and decision making. Various disciplines, such as psychology, philosophy, linguistics, science, and computer science all study cognition. However, the term's usage varies across disciplines; for example, in psychology and cognitive science, 'cognition' usually refers to an information processing view of an individual's psychological functions.
Self-consciousness	Self-consciousness is an acute sense of self-awareness. It is a preoccupation with oneself, as opposed to the philosophical state of self-awareness, which is the awareness that one exists as an individual being; although some writers use both terms interchangeably or synonymously.

Visit Cram101.com for full Practice Exams

Chapter 3. Socialization, the Life Course, and Aging

CHAPTER HIGHLIGHTS & NOTES: KEY TERMS, PEOPLE, PLACES, CONCEPTS

Jean Piaget	Jean Piaget (French pronunciation: ; (9 August 1896 - 16 September 1980) was a Swiss developmental psychologist and philosopher known for his epistemological studies with children. His theory of cognitive development and epistemological view are together called 'genetic epistemology'. Piaget placed great importance on the education of children.
Egocentrism	In psychology, egocentrism is•the incomplete differentiation of the self and the world, including other people and•the tendency to perceive, understand and interpret the world in terms of the self. An egocentric person cannot fully empathize, i.e. 'put himself in other peoples' shoes', and believes everyone sees what she/he sees . In younger children It appears that this egocentric stance towards the world is present mostly in younger children.
Generalized other	The generalized other is a concept introduced by George Herbert Mead into the social sciences, and used especially in the field of symbolic interactionism. It is the general notion that a person has of the common expectations that others have about actions and thoughts within a particular society, and thus serves to clarify their relation to the other as a representative member of a shared social system. Any time that an actor tries to imagine what is expected of them, they are taking on the perspective of the generalized other.
Agent	In economics, an agent is an actor and decision maker in a model. Typically, every agent makes decisions by solving a well or ill defined optimization/choice problem. The term agent can also be seen as equivalent to player in game theory.
Mass media	Mass media refers collectively to all media technologies, including the Internet, television, newspapers, and radio, which are used for mass communications, and to the organizations which control these technologies. Since the 1950s, in the countries that have reached a high level of industrialization, the mass media of cinema, radio and TV have a key role in political power. Mass media play a significant role in shaping public perceptions on a variety of important issues, both through the information that is dispensed through them, and through the interpretations they place upon this information.
Tron	Boris Floricic, better known by his pseudonym Tron (8 June 1972 - 17-22 October 1998), was a German hacker and phreaker whose death in unclear circumstances has led to various conspiracy theories.

Visit Cram101.com for full Practice Exams

Chapter 3. Socialization, the Life Course, and Aging

CHAPTER HIGHLIGHTS & NOTES: KEY TERMS, PEOPLE, PLACES, CONCEPTS

	He is also known for his Diplom thesis presenting one of the first public implementations of a telephone with built-in voice encryption, the 'Cryptophon'. Floricic's pseudonym was a reference to the eponymous character in the 1982 Disney film Tron.
Arranged marriage	An arranged marriage is a practice in which someone other than the couple getting married makes the selection of the persons to be wed, meanwhile curtailing or avoiding the process of courtship. Such marriages had deep roots in royal and aristocratic families around the world. Today, arranged marriage is largely practiced in South Asia (India,Nepal, Pakistan, Bangladesh, Sri Lanka), Africa, the Middle East, and Southeast Asia and East Asia to some extent.
Identity	Identity is a term used to describe a person's conception and expression of their individuality or group affiliations (such as national identity and cultural identity). The term is used more specifically in psychology and sociology, and is given a great deal of attention in social psychology. The term is also used with respect to place identity.
Childhood	Childhood is the age span ranging from birth to adolescence. In developmental psychology, childhood is divided up into the developmental stages of toddlerhood (learning to walk), early childhood middle childhood and adolescence (puberty through post-puberty). The term childhood is non-specific and can imply a varying range of years in human development.
Functionalism	Functionalism is a theory of the mind in contemporary philosophy, developed largely as an alternative to both the identity theory of mind and behaviourism. Its core idea is that mental states (beliefs, desires, being in pain, etc). are constituted solely by their functional role -- that is, they are causal relations to other mental states, sensory inputs, and behavioral outputs.
Activity theory	The activity theory, also known as the implicit theory of aging, normal theory of aging, and lay theory of aging, proposes that successful aging occurs when older adults stay active and maintain social interactions. The activity theory rose in opposing response to the disengagement theory. The activity theory and the disengagement theory were the two major theories that outlined successful aging in the early 1960s.
Social class	Social class is a set of concepts in the social sciences and political theory centered on models of social stratification in which people are grouped into a set of hierarchical social categories. Class is an essential object of analysis for sociologists, political scientists, anthropologists and social historians. However, there is not a consensus on the best definition of the term 'class', and the term has different contextual meanings.

Chapter 3. Socialization, the Life Course, and Aging

CHAPTER HIGHLIGHTS & NOTES: KEY TERMS, PEOPLE, PLACES, CONCEPTS

Social conflict	Social conflict is the struggle for agency or power in society. Social conflict or group conflict occurs when two or more actors oppose each other in social interaction, reciprocally exerting social power in an effort to attain scarce or incompatible goals and prevent the opponent from attaining them. It is a social relationship wherein the action is oriented intentionally for carrying out the actor's own will against the resistance of other party or parties Conflict theory emphasizes interests, rather than norms and values, in conflict.
Baby boomer	A baby boomer is a person who was born during the demographic post-World War II baby boom between the years 1946 and 1964, according to the U.S. Census Bureau. The term 'baby boomer' is sometimes used in a cultural context. Therefore, it is impossible to achieve broad consensus of a precise definition, even within a given territory.
Medicare	Medicare is a national social insurance program, administered by the U.S. federal government in 1965, that guarantees access to health insurance for Americans ages 65 and older and younger people with disabilities as well as people with end stage renal disease. As a social insurance program, Medicare spreads the financial risk associated with illness across society to protect everyone, and thus has a somewhat different social role from private insurers, which must manage their risk portfolio to guarantee their own solvency. Medicare offers all enrollees a defined benefit.
Social security	Social security is a concept enshrined in Article 22 of the Universal Declaration of Human Rights which states that Everyone, as a member of society, has the right to social security and is entitled to realization, through national effort and international co-operation and in accordance with the organization and resources of each State, of the economic, social and cultural rights indispensable for his dignity and the free development of his personality. In simple term, this means that the signatories agree that society in which a person lives should help them to develop and to make the most of all the advantages (culture, work, social welfare) which are offered to them in the country. Social security may also refer to the action programs of government intended to promote the welfare of the population through assistance measures guaranteeing access to sufficient resources for food and shelter and to promote health and wellbeing for the population at large and potentially vulnerable segments such as children, the elderly, the sick and the unemployed.
Health insurance	Health insurance is insurance against the risk of incurring medical expenses. By estimating the overall risk of health care expenses, an insurer can develop a routine finance structure, such as a monthly premium or payroll tax, to ensure that money is available to pay for the health care benefits specified in the insurance agreement.

Chapter 3. Socialization, the Life Course, and Aging

CHAPTER HIGHLIGHTS & NOTES: KEY TERMS, PEOPLE, PLACES, CONCEPTS

Elder abuse	Elder abuse is a general term used to describe certain types of harm to older adults. Other terms commonly used include: 'elder mistreatment', 'senior abuse', 'abuse in later life', 'abuse of older adults', 'abuse of older women', and 'abuse of older men'. One of the more commonly accepted definitions of elder abuse is 'a single, or repeated act, or lack of appropriate action, occurring within any relationship where there is an expectation of trust which causes harm or distress to an older person.' This definition has been adopted by the World Health Organization from a definition put forward by Action on Elder Abuse in the UK. The core feature of this definition is that it focuses on harms where there is 'expectation of trust' of the older person toward their abuser.
Nursing home	A nursing home, convalescent home, Skilled Nursing Unit (SNU), care home or rest home provides a type of care of residents: it is a place of residence for people who require constant nursing care and have significant deficiencies with activities of daily living. Residents include the elderly and younger adults with physical or mental disabilities. Residents in a skilled nursing facility may also receive physical, occupational, and other rehabilitative therapies following an accident or illness.
Social isolation	Social isolation refers to a complete or near-complete lack of contact with society for members of social species. It is usually involuntary, making it distinct from isolating tendencies or actions consciously undertaken by a person, all of which go by various other names. It is also not the same as loneliness rooted in temporary lack of contact with other humans.
Ageism	Ageism is stereotyping and discriminating against individuals or groups because of their age. It is a set of beliefs, attitudes, norms, and values used to justify age based prejudice, discrimination, and subordination. This may be casual or systematic.

Chapter 3. Socialization, the Life Course, and Aging

CHAPTER QUIZ: KEY TERMS, PEOPLE, PLACES, CONCEPTS

1. The _____, also known as the implicit theory of aging, normal theory of aging, and lay theory of aging, proposes that successful aging occurs when older adults stay active and maintain social interactions. The _____ rose in opposing response to the disengagement theory. The _____ and the disengagement theory were the two major theories that outlined successful aging in the early 1960s.

    a. Activity theory
    b. Age and Ageing
    c. Age Concern
    d. Ageism

2. _____ was an American philosopher, sociologist and psychologist, primarily affiliated with the University of Chicago, where he was one of several distinguished pragmatists. He is regarded as one of the founders of social psychology and the American sociological tradition in general.

    Mead was born February 27, 1863 in South Hadley, Massachusetts.

    a. Stanley Milgram
    b. Walter Mischel
    c. George Herbert Mead
    d. John Neulinger

3. An _____ is a practice in which someone other than the couple getting married makes the selection of the persons to be wed, meanwhile curtailing or avoiding the process of courtship. Such marriages had deep roots in royal and aristocratic families around the world. Today, _____ is largely practiced in South Asia (India, Nepal, Pakistan, Bangladesh, Sri Lanka), Africa, the Middle East, and Southeast Asia and East Asia to some extent.

    a. Antonio Commisso
    b. Bergen Newspaper Group
    c. Arranged marriage
    d. DD172

4. . _____ refers collectively to all media technologies, including the Internet, television, newspapers, and radio, which are used for mass communications, and to the organizations which control these technologies.

    Since the 1950s, in the countries that have reached a high level of industrialization, the _____ of cinema, radio and TV have a key role in political power. _____ play a significant role in shaping public perceptions on a variety of important issues, both through the information that is dispensed through them, and through the interpretations they place upon this information.

    a. 352 media group
    b. Bergen Newspaper Group
    c. Mass media

Visit Cram101.com for full Practice Exams

Chapter 3. Socialization, the Life Course, and Aging

CHAPTER QUIZ: KEY TERMS, PEOPLE, PLACES, CONCEPTS

5. In psychology, _____ is the incomplete differentiation of the self and the world, including other people and the tendency to perceive, understand and interpret the world in terms of the self. An egocentric person cannot fully empathize, i.e. 'put himself in other peoples' shoes', and believes everyone sees what she/he sees.

In younger children

It appears that this egocentric stance towards the world is present mostly in younger children.

a. individualism
b. Antonio Commisso
c. Egocentrism
d. Real Boys

Visit Cram101.com for full Practice Exams

ANSWER KEY
Chapter 3. Socialization, the Life Course, and Aging

1. a
2. c
3. c
4. c
5. c

You can take the complete Chapter Practice Test

for Chapter 3. Socialization, the Life Course, and Aging
on all key terms, persons, places, and concepts.

Online 99 Cents

http://www.epub4.5.21549.3.cram101.com/

Use www.Cram101.com for all your study needs

including Cram101's online interactive problem solving labs in

chemistry, statistics, mathematics, and more.

Visit Cram101.com for full Practice Exams

Chapter 4. Social Interaction and Everyday Life in the Age of the Internet

CHAPTER OUTLINE: KEY TERMS, PEOPLE, PLACES, CONCEPTS

- Charles Lindbergh
- Microsociology
- Social interaction
- Social network
- Nonverbal communication
- The Voyage of the Beagle
- Paul Ekman
- Webcam
- Impression management
- Social position
- Eye contact
- Ethnomethodology
- Personal space
- Economic growth
- Sweatshop
- Passing
- Streetwise

Visit Cram101.com for full Practice Exams

Chapter 4. Social Interaction and Everyday Life in the Age of the Internet

CHAPTER HIGHLIGHTS & NOTES: KEY TERMS, PEOPLE, PLACES, CONCEPTS

Charles Lindbergh	Charles Augustus Lindbergh (February 4, 1902 - August 26, 1974) was an American aviator, author, inventor, explorer, and social activist.

As a 25-year-old U.S. Air Mail pilot, Lindbergh emerged from obscurity to virtually instantaneous world fame as the result of his Orteig Prize-winning solo non-stop flight on May 20-21, 1927, from Roosevelt Field located in Garden City on New York's Long Island to Le Bourget Field in Paris, France, a distance of nearly 3,600 statute miles (5,800 km), in the single-seat, single-engine monoplane Spirit of St. Louis. Lindbergh, a U.S. Army reserve officer, was also awarded the nation's highest military decoration, the Medal of Honor, for his historic exploit.

In the late 1920s and early 1930s, Lindbergh used his fame to promote the development of both commercial aviation and Air Mail services in the United States and the Americas. In March 1932, however, his infant son, Charles, Jr., was kidnapped and murdered in what was soon dubbed the 'Crime of the Century'; this led to the Lindbergh family being 'driven into voluntary exile' and fleeing the United States in late December 1935 to live in Europe. The family continued to live overseas until returning to the U.S. in April 1939.

Before the United States formally entered World War II, Lindbergh had been an outspoken advocate of keeping the U.S. out of the world conflict, as had his father, Congressman Charles August Lindbergh, during World War I; Lindbergh even became a leader in the anti-war America First movement. Nonetheless, he supported the war effort after Pearl Harbor and flew many combat missions in the Pacific Theater of World War II as a civilian consultant, as President Franklin D. Roosevelt had refused to reinstate his Army Air Corps colonel's commission that he had resigned in April 1941.

In his later years, Lindbergh became a prolific prize-winning author, international explorer, inventor, and environmentalist. Early years

Charles Augustus Lindbergh was born in Detroit, Michigan, on February 4, 1902, but spent most of his childhood in Little Falls, Minnesota, and Washington, D.C.. He was the only child of Swedish immigrant Charles August Lindbergh (birth name Carl Månsson) (1859-1924), and Evangeline Lodge Land (1876-1954), of Detroit. The Lindberghs separated in 1909. Lindbergh, Sr. was a U.S. Congressman (R-MN 6th) from 1907 to 1917 who gained notoriety when he opposed the entry of the U.S. into World War I. Mrs. Lindbergh was a Chemistry teacher at Cass Technical High School in Detroit and later at Little Falls High School, from which Charles graduated in 1918. Lindbergh also attended over a dozen other schools from Washington, D.C., to California during his childhood and teenage years (none for more than a full year) including the Force School and Sidwell Friends School while living in Washington, D.C., with his father, and Redondo Union High School in Redondo Beach, California. Lindbergh enrolled in the College of Engineering at the University of Wisconsin-Madison in the Fall of 1920, but dropped out in the middle of his sophomore year and headed for Lincoln, Nebraska in March 1922 to begin flight training. Early aviation career |

Chapter 4. Social Interaction and Everyday Life in the Age of the Internet

CHAPTER HIGHLIGHTS & NOTES: KEY TERMS, PEOPLE, PLACES, CONCEPTS

Microsociology	Microsociology is one of the main branches of sociology, concerning the nature of everyday human social interactions and agency on a small scale: face to face. Microsociology is based on interpretative analysis rather than statistical or empirical observation, and shares close association with the philosophy of phenomenology. Methods includes symbolic interactionism and ethnomethodology; ethnomethodology in particular has led to many academic sub-divisions and studies such as microlinguistical research and other related aspects of human social behaviour.
Social interaction	In sociology, social interaction is a dynamic, changing sequence of social actions between individuals (or groups) who modify their actions and reactions due to the actions by their interaction partner(s). Social interactions can be differentiated into accidental, repeated, regular, and regulated. Social interactions form the basis for social relations.
Social network	A social network is a social structure made up of a set of actors (such as individuals or organizations) and the dyadic ties between these actors. The social network perspective provides a clear way of analyzing the structure of whole social entities. The study of these structures usessocial network analysis to identify local and global patterns, locate influential entities, and examine network dynamics.
Nonverbal communication	Nonverbal communication is usually understood as the process of communication through sending and receiving wordless (mostly visual) messages between people. Messages can be communicated through gestures and touch, by body language or posture, by facial expression and eye contact. Nonverbal messages could also be communicated through material exponential; meaning, objects or artifacts (such as clothing, hairstyles or architecture).
The Voyage of the Beagle	The Voyage of the Beagle is a title commonly given to the book written by Charles Darwin and published in 1839 as his Journal and Remarks, bringing him considerable fame and respect. The title refers to the second survey expedition of the ship HMS Beagle, which set sail from Plymouth Sound on 27 December 1831 under the command of Captain Robert FitzRoy, R.N..

While the expedition was originally planned to last two years, it lasted almost five-the Beagle did not return until 2 October 1836. Darwin spent most of this time exploring on land (three years and three months on land; 18 months at sea). |
| Paul Ekman | Paul Ekman is an American psychologist who has been a pioneer in the study of emotions and their relation to facial expressions. He has been considered one of the 100 most eminent psychologists of the twentieth century. The background of Ekman's research analyzes the development of human traits and states over time (Keltner, 2007). |
| Webcam | A webcam is a video camera which feeds its images in real time to a computer or computer network, often via USB, ethernet or Wi-Fi. |

Chapter 4. Social Interaction and Everyday Life in the Age of the Internet

CHAPTER HIGHLIGHTS & NOTES: KEY TERMS, PEOPLE, PLACES, CONCEPTS

	Their most popular use is the establishment of video links, permitting computers to act as videophones or videoconference stations. This common use as a video camera for the World Wide Web gave the webcam its name.
Impression management	In sociology and social psychology, impression management is a goal-directed conscious or unconscious process in which people attempt to influence the perceptions of other people about a person, object or event; they do so by regulating and controlling information in social interaction (Piwinger & Ebert 2001, pp. 1-2). It is usually used synonymously with self-presentation, in which a person tries to influence the perception of their image. The notion of impression management also refers to practices in professional communication and public relations, where the term is used to describe the process of formation of a company's or organization's public image.
Social position	Social position is the position of an individual in a given society and culture. A given position (for example, the occupation of priest) may belong to many individuals. Social position influences social status.
Eye contact	Eye contact is a meeting of the eyes between two individuals. In human beings, eye contact is a form of nonverbal communication and is thought to have a large influence on social behavior. Coined in the early to mid-1960s, the term has come in the West to often define the act as a meaningful and important sign of confidence and social communication.
Ethnomethodology	Ethnomethodology is an ethnographic approach to sociological inquiry introduced by the American sociologist Harold Garfinkel (1917-2011). Ethnomethodology's research interest is the study of the everyday methods people use for the production of social order (Garfinkel:2002). Ethnomethodology's goal is to document the methods and practices through which society's members make sense of their world.
Personal space	Personal space is the region surrounding a person which they regard as psychologically theirs. Invasion of personal space often leads to discomfort, anger, or anxiety on the part of the victim. The notion of personal space comes from Edward T. Hall, whose ideas were influenced by Heini Hediger's studies of behavior of zoo animals.
Economic growth	Economic growth is the increase of per capita gross domestic product (GDP) or other measures of aggregate income, typically reported as the annual rate of change in real GDP. Economic growth is primarily driven by improvements in productivity, which involves producing more goods and services with the same inputs of labour, capital, energy and materials. Economists draw a distinction between short-term economic stabilization and long-term economic growth.

Chapter 4. Social Interaction and Everyday Life in the Age of the Internet

CHAPTER HIGHLIGHTS & NOTES: KEY TERMS, PEOPLE, PLACES, CONCEPTS

Sweatshop	Sweatshop is a negatively connoted term for any working environment considered to be unacceptably difficult or dangerous. Sweatshop workers often work long hours for very low pay, regardless of laws mandating overtime pay or a minimum wage. Child labour laws may be violated.
Passing	Passing is the ability of a person to be regarded as a member of social groups other than his or her own, such as a different race, ethnicity, social class, gender, intelligence, age and/or disability status, generally with the purpose of gaining social acceptance.
Streetwise	Streetwise may refer to:•Rover Streetwise, a small hatchback made by the MG Rover Group•Knowledge of youth culture, also called 'street'•Practical knowledge, as opposed to ivory tower or book knowledge, knowledge on how to succeed through life, or generally how to avoid the pitfalls•The Streetwise Fund, a mutual fund offered by ING Direct In media•StreetWise, a Chicago newspaper•Street Smarts (game show), a TV game show•Streetwise a 1984 documentary following the lives of homeless teenagers living on the streets of downtown Seattle•Streetwise a 1998 film•Streetwise the name of several Transformers characters.

CHAPTER QUIZ: KEY TERMS, PEOPLE, PLACES, CONCEPTS

1. In sociology, _____ is a dynamic, changing sequence of social actions between individuals (or groups) who modify their actions and reactions due to the actions by their interaction partner(s). _____s can be differentiated into accidental, repeated, regular, and regulated. _____s form the basis for social relations.

    a. Senior citizen
    b. Value-rational action
    c. Social interaction
    d. Social order

2. . Charles Augustus Lindbergh (February 4, 1902 - August 26, 1974) was an American aviator, author, inventor, explorer, and social activist.

    As a 25-year-old U.S. Air Mail pilot, Lindbergh emerged from obscurity to virtually instantaneous world fame as the result of his Orteig Prize-winning solo non-stop flight on May 20-21, 1927, from Roosevelt Field located in Garden City on New York's Long Island to Le Bourget Field in Paris, France, a distance of nearly 3,600 statute miles (5,800 km), in the single-seat, single-engine monoplane Spirit of St. Louis. Lindbergh, a U.S. Army reserve officer, was also awarded the nation's highest military decoration, the Medal of Honor, for his historic exploit.

Visit Cram101.com for full Practice Exams

Chapter 4. Social Interaction and Everyday Life in the Age of the Internet

CHAPTER QUIZ: KEY TERMS, PEOPLE, PLACES, CONCEPTS

In the late 1920s and early 1930s, Lindbergh used his fame to promote the development of both commercial aviation and Air Mail services in the United States and the Americas. In March 1932, however, his infant son, Charles, Jr., was kidnapped and murdered in what was soon dubbed the 'Crime of the Century'; this led to the Lindbergh family being 'driven into voluntary exile' and fleeing the United States in late December 1935 to live in Europe. The family continued to live overseas until returning to the U.S. in April 1939.

Before the United States formally entered World War II, Lindbergh had been an outspoken advocate of keeping the U.S. out of the world conflict, as had his father, Congressman Charles August Lindbergh, during World War I; Lindbergh even became a leader in the anti-war America First movement. Nonetheless, he supported the war effort after Pearl Harbor and flew many combat missions in the Pacific Theater of World War II as a civilian consultant, as President Franklin D. Roosevelt had refused to reinstate his Army Air Corps colonel's commission that he had resigned in April 1941.

In his later years, Lindbergh became a prolific prize-winning author, international explorer, inventor, and environmentalist. Early years

Charles Augustus Lindbergh was born in Detroit, Michigan, on February 4, 1902, but spent most of his childhood in Little Falls, Minnesota, and Washington, D.C.. He was the only child of Swedish immigrant Charles August Lindbergh (birth name Carl Månsson) (1859-1924), and Evangeline Lodge Land (1876-1954), of Detroit. The Lindberghs separated in 1909. Lindbergh, Sr. was a U.S. Congressman (R-MN 6th) from 1907 to 1917 who gained notoriety when he opposed the entry of the U.S. into World War I. Mrs. Lindbergh was a Chemistry teacher at Cass Technical High School in Detroit and later at Little Falls High School, from which Charles graduated in 1918. Lindbergh also attended over a dozen other schools from Washington, D.C., to California during his childhood and teenage years (none for more than a full year) including the Force School and Sidwell Friends School while living in Washington, D.C., with his father, and Redondo Union High School in Redondo Beach, California. Lindbergh enrolled in the College of Engineering at the University of Wisconsin-Madison in the Fall of 1920, but dropped out in the middle of his sophomore year and headed for Lincoln, Nebraska in March 1922 to begin flight training. Early aviation career

From an early age _____ had exhibited an interest in the mechanics of motorized transportation including his family's Saxon Six automobile, and later his Excelsior motorbike.

a. Wilhelm Marr
b. Charles Lindbergh
c. Metapedia
d. Miscegenation

3. . _____ is one of the main branches of sociology, concerning the nature of everyday human social interactions and agency on a small scale: face to face. _____ is based on interpretative analysis rather than statistical or empirical observation, and shares close association with the philosophy of phenomenology. Methods includes symbolic interactionism and ethnomethodology; ethnomethodology in particular has led to many academic sub-divisions and studies such as microlinguistical research and other related aspects of human social behaviour.

Chapter 4. Social Interaction and Everyday Life in the Age of the Internet

CHAPTER QUIZ: KEY TERMS, PEOPLE, PLACES, CONCEPTS

   a. Microsociology
   b. Sociology of punishment
   c. Sociology of scientific knowledge
   d. Sociography

4. _____ is a meeting of the eyes between two individuals.

   In human beings, _____ is a form of nonverbal communication and is thought to have a large influence on social behavior. Coined in the early to mid-1960s, the term has come in the West to often define the act as a meaningful and important sign of confidence and social communication.

   a. Eye contact
   b. Antonio Commisso
   c. Antonio Imerti
   d. Three-component theory of stratification

5. A _____ is a social structure made up of a set of actors (such as individuals or organizations) and the dyadic ties between these actors. The _____ perspective provides a clear way of analyzing the structure of whole social entities. The study of these structures uses _____ analysis to identify local and global patterns, locate influential entities, and examine network dynamics.

   a. Social reality
   b. Social rule system theory
   c. Social threefolding
   d. Social network

Visit Cram101.com for full Practice Exams

ANSWER KEY
Chapter 4. Social Interaction and Everyday Life in the Age of the Internet

1. c
2. b
3. a
4. a
5. d

You can take the complete Chapter Practice Test

for Chapter 4. Social Interaction and Everyday Life in the Age of the Internet
on all key terms, persons, places, and concepts.

Online 99 Cents

http://www.epub4.5.21549.4.cram101.com/

Use www.Cram101.com for all your study needs

including Cram101's online interactive problem solving labs in

chemistry, statistics, mathematics, and more.

Chapter 5. Groups, Networks, and Organizations

CHAPTER OUTLINE: KEY TERMS, PEOPLE, PLACES, CONCEPTS

_____ Social group

_____ Out-group

_____ Secondary group

_____ Georg Simmel

_____ Dyad

_____ Triad

_____ Nelson Mandela

_____ Conformity

_____ Stanley Milgram

_____ Obedience

_____ Bay of Pigs Invasion

_____ Social network

_____ Corporation

_____ Bureaucracy

_____ Ideal type

_____ John W. Meyer

_____ Iron law of oligarchy

_____ Oligarchy

_____ Holocaust

Visit Cram101.com for full Practice Exams

Chapter 5. Groups, Networks, and Organizations

CHAPTER OUTLINE: KEY TERMS, PEOPLE, PLACES, CONCEPTS

_____	Entrepreneurial culture
_____	Human resource management
_____	Telecommuting
_____	Robert D. Putnam
_____	Civic engagement
_____	Social capital
_____	Bowling Alone
_____	National Organization for Women
_____	Voter turnout

CHAPTER HIGHLIGHTS & NOTES: KEY TERMS, PEOPLE, PLACES, CONCEPTS

Social group	In the social sciences a social group is two or more humans who interact with one another, share similar characteristics and collectively have a sense of unity, although the best way to define social group is a matter of conjecture. Regardless, a society can be viewed as a large group, though most social groups are considerably smaller. Society can also be viewed as people who interact with one another, sharing similarities pertaining to culture and territorial boundaries.
Out-group	In sociology, an out-group is a social group towards which an individual feels contempt, opposition, or a desire to compete. Members of outgroups may be subject to outgroup homogeneity biases, and generally people tend to privilege ingroup members over outgroup members in many situations. The term originates from social identity theory.
Secondary group	People in a secondary group interact on a less personal level than in a primary group, and their relationships are temporary rather than long lasting.

Visit Cram101.com for full Practice Exams

Chapter 5. Groups, Networks, and Organizations

CHAPTER HIGHLIGHTS & NOTES: KEY TERMS, PEOPLE, PLACES, CONCEPTS

	Since secondary groups are established to perform functions, people's roles are more interchangeable. A secondary group is one you have chosen to be a part of. They are based on interests and activities.
Georg Simmel	Georg Simmel was a German sociologist, philosopher, and critic. Georg Simmel was one of the first generation of German sociologists: his neo-Kantian approach laid the foundations for sociological antipositivism, asking 'What is society?' in a direct allusion to Kant's question 'What is nature?', presenting pioneering analyses of social individuality and fragmentation. For Georg Simmel, culture referred to 'the cultivation of individuals through the agency of external forms which have been objectified in the course of history'.
Dyad	In sociology, a dyad is a group of two people, the smallest possible social group. As an adjective, 'dyadic' describes their interaction. The pair of individuals in a dyad can be linked via romantic interest, family relation, interests, work, partners in crime and so on.
Triad	Triad is a term used to describe many branches of Chinese criminal organizations based in Hong Kong, Vietnam, Macau, Taiwan, China, and also in countries with significant Chinese populations, such as Malaysia, Singapore, the United States, Canada, Australia, New Zealand and the United Kingdom. The Chinese triads are one of the world's largest criminal organizations, encompassing other criminal organizations with a steady membership of around 1.5 million in mainland China alone and 2.5 million members worldwide. Precursors The earliest triads started as resistance/rebel forces who opposed Manchu rule in China during the Qing Dynasty, as the Manchu ethnic group were regarded as foreign invaders in the predominant Han Chinese society of China then.
Nelson Mandela	Nelson Mandela is a South African politician who served as President of South Africa from 1994 to 1999, the first ever to be elected in a fully representative democratic election. Before being elected President, Nelson Mandela was a militant anti-apartheid activist, and the leader and co-founder of Umkhonto we Sizwe, the armed wing of the African National Congress (ANC). In 1962 he was arrested and convicted of sabotage and other charges, and sentenced to life imprisonment.
Conformity	Conformity is the act of matching attitudes, beliefs, and behaviors to group norms. Norms are implicit rules shared by a group of individuals, that guide their interactions with others and among society or social group.

Chapter 5. Groups, Networks, and Organizations

CHAPTER HIGHLIGHTS & NOTES: KEY TERMS, PEOPLE, PLACES, CONCEPTS

Stanley Milgram	Stanley Milgram was an American social psychologist most notable for his controversial study known as the Milgram Experiment. The study was conducted in the 1960s during Milgram's professorship at Yale. Milgram was influenced by the events of the Nazi Holocaust to carry out an experiment that would demonstrate the relationship between obedience and authority.
Obedience	In human behavior, obedience is 'a form of social influence in which a person yields to explicit instructions or orders from an authority figure' (Coleman,2006)]] Obedience differs from compliance, which is behavior influenced by peers, and from conformity, which is behavior intended to match that of the majority. Obedience can be seen as both a sin and a virtue. For example in a situation when one orders a person to kill another innocent person and he or she does this willingly, it is a sin.
Bay of Pigs Invasion	The Bay of Pigs Invasion was an unsuccessful action by a CIA-trained force of Cuban exiles to invade southern Cuba, with support and encouragement from the US government, in an attempt to overthrow the Cuban government of Fidel Castro. The invasion was launched in April 1961, less than three months after John F. Kennedy assumed the presidency in the United States. The Cuban armed forces, trained and equipped by Eastern Bloc nations, defeated the invading combatants within three days.
Social network	A social network is a social structure made up of a set of actors (such as individuals or organizations) and the dyadic ties between these actors. The social network perspective provides a clear way of analyzing the structure of whole social entities. The study of these structures usessocial network analysis to identify local and global patterns, locate influential entities, and examine network dynamics.
Corporation	A corporation is an incorporated entity is a separate legal entity that has been incorporated through a legislative or registration process established through legislation. Incorporated entities have legal rights and liabilities that are distinct from its shareholders, and may conduct business for either profit-seeking business or not for profit purposes. Early incorporated entities were established by charter (i.e. by an ad hoc act granted by a monarch or passed by a parliament or legislature).
Bureaucracy	A bureaucracy is an organization of non-elected officials of a government or organization who implements the rules, laws, and functions of their institution. Bureaucracies date back to ancient societies across the globe. Pre-Modern World Modern world Weberian bureaucracy

Chapter 5. Groups, Networks, and Organizations

CHAPTER HIGHLIGHTS & NOTES: KEY TERMS, PEOPLE, PLACES, CONCEPTS

Ideal type	Ideal type, is a typological term most closely associated with antipositivist sociologist Max Weber (1864-1920). For Weber, the conduct of social science depends upon the construction of hypothetical concepts in the abstract. The 'ideal type' is therefore a subjective element in social theory and research; one of many subjective elements which necessarily distinguish sociology from natural science.
John W. Meyer	John W. Meyer is a sociologist and professor at Stanford University, located in Palo Alto, California, noted for his contributions to the study of organizations, diffusion, and modern mass education. He is best known in sociology for the development of the neo-institutional perspective on globalization, known as world society or world polity theory. He received his B.A. in Psychology from Goshen College, located in Goshen, Indiana in 1955, his M.A. in Sociology from the University of Colorado in 1957, and his Ph.D. in Sociology from Columbia University in 1965. Since 1966, he has been a professor at Stanford University (emeritus since 2001).
Iron law of oligarchy	The iron law of oligarchy is a political theory, first developed by the German syndicalist sociologist Robert Michels in his 1911 book, Political Parties. It claims that rule by an elite - or 'oligarchy' is inevitable as an 'iron law' within any organization as part of the 'tactical and technical necessities' of organization. Michels particularly addressed the application of this law to democracy, and stated: 'It is organization which gives birth to the dominion of the elected over the electors, of the mandataries over the mandators, of the delegates over the delegators.
Oligarchy	Oligarchy (from Greek ?λιγαρχ?α (oligarkhía); from ?λ?γος (olígos), meaning 'a few', and ?ρχω (archo), meaning 'to rule or to command') is a form of power structure in which power effectively rests with a small number of people. These people could be distinguished by royalty, wealth, family ties, education, corporate, or military control. Such states are often controlled by a few prominent families who pass their influence from one generation to the next.
Holocaust	The Holocaust also known as the Shoah, was the mass murder or genocide of approximately six million Jews during World War II, a programme of systematic state-sponsored murder by Nazi Germany, led by Adolf Hitler and the Nazi Party, throughout German-occupied territory. Of the nine million Jews who had resided in Europe before the Holocaust, approximately two-thirds were killed. Over one million Jewish children were killed in the Holocaust, as were approximately two million Jewish women and three million Jewish men.
Entrepreneurial culture	Entrepreneurial culture, is a form of ideal, which is based on the value system of an enterprise and closely related to the management philosophy as well as the management behaviour of the enterprise. It is where the kernel of business management lies.

Chapter 5. Groups, Networks, and Organizations

CHAPTER HIGHLIGHTS & NOTES: KEY TERMS, PEOPLE, PLACES, CONCEPTS

Human resource management	Human resource management is the management of an organization's workforce, or human resources. It is responsible for the attraction, selection, training, assessment, and rewarding of employees, while also overseeing organizational leadership and culture, and ensuring compliance with employment and labor laws. In circumstances where employees desire and are legally authorized to hold a collective bargaining agreement, HR will typically also serve as the company's primary liaison with the employees' representatives (usually a labor union).
Telecommuting	Telecommuting is a work arrangement in which employees enjoy flexibility in working location and hours. In other words, the daily commute to a central place of work is replaced by telecommunication links. Many work from home, while others, occasionally also referred to as nomad workers or web commuters utilize mobile telecommunications technology to work from coffee shops or other locations.
Robert D. Putnam	Robert David Putnam is a political scientist and professor of public policy at the Harvard University John F. Kennedy School of Government. He is also visiting professor and director of the Manchester Graduate Summer Programme in Social Change, University of Manchester (UK). Putnam developed the influential two-level game theory that assumes international agreements will only be successfully brokered if they also result in domestic benefits. His most famous (and controversial) work, Bowling Alone, argues that the United States has undergone an unprecedented collapse in civic, social, associational, and political life (social capital) since the 1960s, with serious negative consequences. Putnam graduated from Swarthmore College in 1963, won a Fulbright Fellowship to study at Balliol College, Oxford, and went on to earn master's and doctorate degrees from Yale University, the latter in 1970. He taught at the University of Michigan until going to Harvard in 1979, where he has held a variety of positions, including Dean of the Kennedy School, and is currently the Malkin Professor of Public Policy. Putnam was raised as a religiously observant Methodist. Around the time of his marriage, he converted to Judaism, his wife's religion. His first work in the area of social capital was Making Democracy Work: Civic Traditions in Modern Italy, a comparative study of regional governments in Italy which drew great scholarly attention for its argument that the success of democracies depends in large part on the horizontal bonds that make up social capital. 'Bowling Alone' and its critics In 1995 he published 'Bowling Alone: America's Declining Social Capital' in the Journal of Democracy Some critics argued that Putnam was ignoring new organizations and forms of social capital; others argued that many of the included organizations were responsible for the suppression of civil rights movements and the reinforcement of anti-egalitarian social norms. Over the last decade and a half, the United States had seen an increase in bowlers but a decrease in bowling leagues.

Chapter 5. Groups, Networks, and Organizations

CHAPTER HIGHLIGHTS & NOTES: KEY TERMS, PEOPLE, PLACES, CONCEPTS

In 2000, he published Bowling Alone: The Collapse and Revival of American Community, a book-length expansion of the original argument, adding new evidence and answering many of his critics. Though he measured the decline of social capital with data of many varieties, his most striking point was that many traditional civic, social and fraternal organizations -- typified by bowling leagues -- had undergone a massive decline in membership while the number of people bowling had increased dramatically.

Putnam makes a distinction between two kinds of social capital: bonding capital and bridging capital. Bonding occurs when you are socializing with people who are like you: same age, same race, same religion, and so on. But in order to create peaceful societies in a diverse multi-ethnic country, one needs to have a second kind of social capital: bridging. Bridging is what you do when you make friends with people who are not like you, like supporters of another football team. Putnam argues that those two kinds of social capital, bonding and bridging, do strengthen each other. Consequently, with the decline of the bonding capital mentioned above inevitably comes the decline of the bridging capital leading to greater ethnic tensions.

Critics such as sociologist Claude Fischer argue that (a) Putnam concentrates on organizational forms of social capital, and pays much less attention to networks of interpersonal social capital; (b) neglects the emergence of new forms of supportive organizations on and off the Internet; and (c) the 1960s are a misleading baseline because the era had an unusually high number of traditional organizations.

Since the publication of Bowling Alone, Putnam has worked on efforts to revive American social capital, notably through the Saguaro Seminar, a series of meetings among academics, civil society leaders, commentators, and politicians to discuss strategies to re-connect Americans with their communities. These resulted in the publication of the book and website, Better Together, which provides case studies of vibrant and new forms of social capital building in the United StatesDiversity and trust within communities

In recent years, Putnam has been engaged in a comprehensive study of the relationship between trust within communities and their ethnic diversity. His conclusion based on over 40 cases and 30 000 people within the United States is that, other things being equal, more diversity in a community is associated with less trust both between and within ethnic groups. Although limited to American data, it puts into question both the contact hypothesis and conflict theory in inter-ethnic relations. According to conflict theory, distrust between the ethnic groups will rise with diversity, but not within a group. In contrast, contact theory proposes that distrust will decline as members of different ethnic groups get to know and interact with each other. Putnam describes people of all races, sex, socioeconomic statuses, and ages as 'hunkering down,' avoiding engagement with their local community--both among different ethnic groups and within their own ethnic group.

Chapter 5. Groups, Networks, and Organizations

CHAPTER HIGHLIGHTS & NOTES: KEY TERMS, PEOPLE, PLACES, CONCEPTS

Even when controlling for income inequality and crime rates, two factors which conflict theory states should be the prime causal factors in declining inter-ethnic group trust, more diversity is still associated with less communal trust.

Lowered trust in areas with high diversity is also associated with:•Lower confidence in local government, local leaders and the local news media.•Lower political efficacy - that is, confidence in one's own influence.•Lower frequency of registering to vote, but more interest and knowledge about politics and more participation in protest marches and social reform groups.•Higher political advocacy, but lower expectations that it will bring about a desirable result.•Less expectation that others will cooperate to solve dilemmas of collective action (e.g., voluntary conservation to ease a water or energy shortage).•Less likelihood of working on a community project.•Less likelihood of giving to charity or volunteering.•Fewer close friends and confidants.•Less happiness and lower perceived quality of life.•More time spent watching television and more agreement that 'television is my most important form of entertainment'.

Putnam published his data set from this study in 2001 and subsequently published the full paper in 2007.

Putnam has been criticized for the lag between his initial study and his publication of his article In 2007, writing in City Journal, John Leo questioned whether this suppression of publication was ethical behavior for a scholar, noting that 'Academics aren't supposed to withhold negative data until they can suggest antidotes to their findings.' On the other hand, Putnam did release the data in 2001 and publicized this fact. The proposals that the paper contains are located in a section called 'Becoming Comfortable with Diversity' at the end of his article. This section has been criticized for lacking the rigor of the preceding sections. According to Ilana Mercer 'Putnam concludes the gloomy facts with a stern pep talk'. Recognition

Robert Putnam has been elected a fellow of the American Academy of Arts and Sciences (1980), and a member of the Council on Foreign Relations (1981), the National Academy of Sciences (2001), and the American Philosophical Society (2005). He was the President of the American Political Science Association (2001-2002). He has received honorary degrees from Stockholm University, Ohio State University, University of Antwerp, University of Edinburgh, and LUISS Guido Carli (Rome) among others. He is the recipient of the Wilbur Cross Medal of Yale Graduate School of Arts and Sciences for outstanding career achievement (2003). In 2006 Robert Putnam received the Johan Skytte Prize for the most valuable contribution to political science. Published works •The Beliefs of Politicians: Ideology, Conflict, and Democracy in Britain and Italy (1973)•The Comparative Study of Political Elites (1976)•Bureaucrats and Politicians in Western Democracies (with Joel D. Aberbach and Bert A. Rockman, 1981)•Hanging Together: Cooperation and Conflict in the Seven-Power Summits (with Nicholas Bayne, 1984, revised 1987)•Diplomacy and Domestic Politics: The Logic of Two-Level Games. International Organization.

Chapter 5. Groups, Networks, and Organizations

CHAPTER HIGHLIGHTS & NOTES: KEY TERMS, PEOPLE, PLACES, CONCEPTS

	42 (Summer 1988): 427-460.•Making Democracy Work: Civic Traditions in Modern Italy (with Robert Leonardi and Raffaella Nanetti, 1993)•Bowling Alone: The Collapse and Revival of American Community (2000)•Democracies in Flux: The Evolution of Social Capital in Contemporary Society (Edited by Robert D. Putnam), Oxford University Press, (2002)•Better Together: Restoring the American Community (with Lewis M. Feldstein, 2003)•'E Pluribus Unum: Diversity and Community in the Twenty-first Century -- The 2006 Johan Skytte Prize.' Scandinavian Political Studies 30 (2), June 2007•Age of Obama (co-written with Tom Clark and Edward Fieldhouse), Manchester University Press (2010)•American Grace: How Religion Divides and Unites Us (co-written with David Campbell), Simon & Schuster (2010).
Civic engagement	Civic engagement or civic participation has been defined as 'Individual and collective actions designed to identify and address issues of public concern.' Civic engagement can take many forms-- from individual volunteerism to organizational involvement to electoral participation. It can include efforts to directly address an issue, work with others in a community to solve a problem or interact with the institutions of representative democracy. Another way of describing this concept is the sense of personal responsibility individuals should feel to uphold their obligations as part of any community.
Social capital	In sociology, social capital is the expected collective or economic benefits derived from the preferential treatment and cooperation between individuals and groups. Although different social sciences emphasize different aspects of social capital, they tend to share the core idea 'that social networks have value'. Just as a screwdriver (physical capital) or a university education (human capital) can increase productivity (both individual and collective), so do social contacts affect the productivity of individuals and groups'.
Bowling Alone	Bowling Alone: The Collapse and Revival of American Community (2000, ISBN 0-7432-0304-6) is a book by Robert D. Putnam. It was originally a 1995 essay entitled Bowling Alone: America's Declining Social Capital. Summary In Bowling Alone: America's Declining Social Capital (1995) Putnam surveys the decline of 'social capital' in the United States of America since 1950. He has described the reduction in all the forms of in-person social intercourse upon which Americans used to found, educate, and enrich the fabric of their social lives.

Chapter 5. Groups, Networks, and Organizations

CHAPTER HIGHLIGHTS & NOTES: KEY TERMS, PEOPLE, PLACES, CONCEPTS

National Organization for Women	The National Organization for Women is the largest feminist organization in the United States. It was founded in 1966 and has a membership of 500,000 contributing members. The organization consists of 550 chapters in all 50 U.S. states and the District of Columbia.
Voter turnout	Voter turnout is the percentage of eligible voters who cast a ballot in an election. After increasing for many decades, there has been a trend of decreasing voter turnout in most established democracies since the 1960s. In general, low turnout may be due to disenchantment, indifference, or contentment.

CHAPTER QUIZ: KEY TERMS, PEOPLE, PLACES, CONCEPTS

1. People in a _____ interact on a less personal level than in a primary group, and their relationships are temporary rather than long lasting. Since _____s are established to perform functions, people's roles are more interchangeable. A _____ is one you have chosen to be a part of. They are based on interests and activities.

    a. Group work
    b. Crowd
    c. Secondary group
    d. Bay Area SEG

2. _____ is a work arrangement in which employees enjoy flexibility in working location and hours. In other words, the daily commute to a central place of work is replaced by telecommunication links. Many work from home, while others, occasionally also referred to as nomad workers or web commuters utilize mobile telecommunications technology to work from coffee shops or other locations.

    a. TGIF
    b. Time and attendance
    c. Time clock
    d. Telecommuting

3. . _____: The Collapse and Revival of American Community (2000, ISBN 0-7432-0304-6) is a book by Robert D. Putnam. It was originally a 1995 essay entitled _____: America's Declining Social Capital.

    Summary

    In _____: America's Declining Social Capital (1995) Putnam surveys the decline of 'social capital' in the United States of America since 1950. He has described the reduction in all the forms of in-person social intercourse upon which Americans used to found, educate, and enrich the fabric of their social lives.

Visit Cram101.com for full Practice Exams

Chapter 5. Groups, Networks, and Organizations

CHAPTER QUIZ: KEY TERMS, PEOPLE, PLACES, CONCEPTS

  a. Cafe church
  b. Celebrating the Third Place
  c. Bowling Alone
  d. Chain Reaction 2008

4. In the social sciences a _____ is two or more humans who interact with one another, share similar characteristics and collectively have a sense of unity, although the best way to define _____ is a matter of conjecture. Regardless, a society can be viewed as a large group, though most _____s are considerably smaller. Society can also be viewed as people who interact with one another, sharing similarities pertaining to culture and territorial boundaries.

  a. Social group
  b. Beatnik
  c. Bee
  d. Bogan

5. The _____ also known as the Shoah, was the mass murder or genocide of approximately six million Jews during World War II, a programme of systematic state-sponsored murder by Nazi Germany, led by Adolf Hitler and the Nazi Party, throughout German-occupied territory. Of the nine million Jews who had resided in Europe before the _____, approximately two-thirds were killed. Over one million Jewish children were killed in the _____, as were approximately two million Jewish women and three million Jewish men.

  a. Visa overstay
  b. Social rule system theory
  c. Social threefolding
  d. Holocaust

ANSWER KEY
Chapter 5. Groups, Networks, and Organizations

1. c
2. d
3. c
4. a
5. d

You can take the complete Chapter Practice Test

for Chapter 5. Groups, Networks, and Organizations
on all key terms, persons, places, and concepts.

Online 99 Cents

http://www.epub4.5.21549.5.cram101.com/

Use www.Cram101.com for all your study needs

including Cram101's online interactive problem solving labs in

chemistry, statistics, mathematics, and more.

Chapter 6. conformity, Deviance, and Crime

CHAPTER OUTLINE: KEY TERMS, PEOPLE, PLACES, CONCEPTS

- Incarceration
- Norm
- Deviance
- Cesare Lombroso
- Anomie
- Kingsley Davis
- Prostitution
- Albert K. Cohen
- Differential association
- Opportunity cost
- Reinforcement
- Reinforcement theory
- Social control theory
- Attachment
- Counterculture
- Howard S. Becker
- Black Power
- Labeling theory
- White-collar crime

Visit Cram101.com for full Practice Exams

Chapter 6. conformity, Deviance, and Crime
CHAPTER OUTLINE: KEY TERMS, PEOPLE, PLACES, CONCEPTS

_____ Primary deviance

_____ Secondary deviance

_____ Self-fulfilling prophecy

_____ National Crime Victimization Survey

_____ Property crime

_____ Gender crime

_____ Crime statistics

_____ Binge drinking

_____ Mass murder

_____ Crack cocaine

_____ Ecstasy

_____ Arranged marriage

_____ Heroin

_____ Corporate crime

_____ Organized crime

_____ Costs

_____ Prison

_____ Knowledge worker

_____ Broken windows theory

Visit Cram101.com for full Practice Exams

Chapter 6. conformity, Deviance, and Crime

CHAPTER OUTLINE: KEY TERMS, PEOPLE, PLACES, CONCEPTS

	Community policing
	Target hardening
	John Braithwaite
	Reintegrative shaming

CHAPTER HIGHLIGHTS & NOTES: KEY TERMS, PEOPLE, PLACES, CONCEPTS

Incarceration	Incarceration is the detention of a person in prison, typically as punishment for a crime (custodial sentence).
	People are most commonly incarcerated upon suspicion or conviction of committing a crime, and different jurisdictions have differing laws governing the function of incarceration within a larger system of justice. Incarceration serves four essential purposes with regard to criminals:•to isolate criminals to prevent them from committing more crimes•to punish criminals for committing crimes•to deter others from committing crimes•to rehabilitate criminals
	Incarceration rates, when measured by the United Nations, are considered distinct and separate from the imprisonment of political prisoners and others not charged with a specific crime.
Norm	Social norms are the behaviors and cues within a society or group. This sociological term has been defined as 'the rules that a group uses for appropriate and inappropriate values, beliefs, attitudes and behaviors. These rules may be explicit or implicit.
Deviance	Deviance, in a sociological context, describes actions or behaviors that violate social norms, including formally-enacted rules (e.g., crime), as well as informal violations of social norms (e.g., rejecting folkways and mores). It is the purview of sociologists, psychologists, psychiatrists, and criminologists to study how these norms are created, how they change over time and how they are enforced.
	Norms are rules and expectations by which members of society are conventionally guided.

Visit Cram101.com for full Practice Exams

Chapter 6. conformity, Deviance, and Crime

CHAPTER HIGHLIGHTS & NOTES: KEY TERMS, PEOPLE, PLACES, CONCEPTS

Cesare Lombroso	Cesare Lombroso, born Ezechia Marco Lombroso was an Italian criminologist and physician, founder of the Italian School of Positivist Criminology. Lombroso rejected the established Classical School, which held that crime was a characteristic trait of human nature. Instead, using concepts drawn from physiognomy, early eugenics, psychiatry and Social Darwinism, Lombroso's theory of anthropological criminology essentially stated that criminality was inherited, and that someone 'born criminal' could be identified by physical defects, which confirmed a criminal as savage, or atavistic.
Anomie	Anomie is a sociological term meaning 'personal feeling of a lack of social norms; normlessness'. It describes the breakdown of social norms and values. It was popularized by French sociologist Émile Durkheim in his influential book Suicide (1897).
Kingsley Davis	Kingsley Davis identified by the American Philosophical Society as one of the most outstanding social scientists of the twentieth century, was a Hoover Institution senior research fellow and internationally recognized American sociologist and demographer. He led and conducted major studies of societies in Europe, South America, Africa and Asia, coined the term 'population explosion,', and played a major role in the naming and development of the demographic transition model. He is also credited with coining the term 'zero population growth' although George Stolnitz claimed to have that distinction.
Prostitution	Prostitution is the act or practice of providing sexual services to another person in return for payment. People who execute such activities are called prostitutes. Prostitution is one of the branches of the sex industry.
Albert K. Cohen	Albert K. Cohen. is a prominent American criminologist. He is known for his Subcultural Theory of delinquent urban gangs, including his influential book Delinquent Boys: Culture of the Gang.
Differential association	In criminology, Differential Association is a theory developed by Edwin Sutherland proposing that through interaction with others, individuals learn the values, attitudes, techniques, and motives for criminal behavior. The Differential Association Theory is the most talked about of the Learning Theories of deviance. This theory focuses on how individuals learn to become criminals, but does not concern itself with why they become criminals.
Opportunity cost	Opportunity cost is the cost of any activity measured in terms of the value of the next best alternative forgone (that is not chosen). It is the sacrifice related to the second best choice available to someone, or group, who has picked among several mutually exclusive choices. The opportunity cost is also the 'cost' (as a lost benefit) of the forgone products after making a choice.

Chapter 6. conformity, Deviance, and Crime

CHAPTER HIGHLIGHTS & NOTES: KEY TERMS, PEOPLE, PLACES, CONCEPTS

Reinforcement	Reinforcement is a term in operant conditioning and behavior analysis for a process of strengthening a directly measurable dimension of behavior-such as rate (e.g., pulling a lever more frequently), duration (e.g., pulling a lever for longer periods of time), magnitude (e.g., pulling a lever with greater force), or latency (e.g., pulling a lever more quickly following the onset of an environmental event)-as a function of the delivery of a stimulus (e.g. money from a slot machine) immediately or shortly after the occurrence of the behavior. Giving a monkey a banana for performing a trick is an example of positive reinforcement. Reinforcement is only said to have occurred if the delivery of the stimulus is directly caused by the response made.
Reinforcement theory	Reinforcement theory is a limited effects media model applicable within the realm of communication. The theory generally states that people seek out and remember information that provides cognitive support for their pre-existing attitudes and beliefs. The main assumption that guides this theory is that people do not like to be wrong and often feel uncomfortable when their beliefs are challenged.
Social control theory	In criminology, social control theory proposes that exploiting the process of socialization and social learning builds self-control and reduces the inclination to indulge in behavior recognized as antisocial. It was derived from Functionalist theories of crime and Ivan Nye (1958) proposed that there are four types of control:•Direct: by which punishment is threatened or applied for wrongful behavior, and compliance is rewarded by parents, family, and authority figures.•Internal: by which a youth refrains from delinquency through the conscience or superego.•Indirect: by identification with those who influence behavior, say because his or her delinquent act might cause pain and disappointment to parents and others with whom he or she has close relationships.•Control through needs satisfaction, i.e. if all an individual's needs are met, there is no point in criminal activity. Discussion Social control theory proposes that people's relationships, commitments, values, norms, and beliefs encourage them not to break the law. Thus, if moral codes are internalized and individuals are tied into, and have a stake in their wider community, they will voluntarily limit their propensity to commit deviant acts.
Attachment	Attachment is a legal process by which a court of law, at the request of a creditor, designates specific property owned by the debtor to be transferred to the creditor, or sold for the benefit of the creditor. A wide variety of legal mechanisms are employed by debtors to prevent the attachment of their assets. For example, a declaration of bankruptcy will severely limit the ability of creditors to attach the property of the debtor.

Chapter 6. conformity, Deviance, and Crime

CHAPTER HIGHLIGHTS & NOTES: KEY TERMS, PEOPLE, PLACES, CONCEPTS

Counterculture	Counterculture is a sociological term used to describe the values and norms of behavior of a cultural group, or subculture, that run counter to those of the social mainstream of the day, the cultural equivalent of political opposition. It is a neologism attributed to Theodore Roszak. Although distinct countercultural undercurrents have existed in many societies, here the term refers to a more significant, visible phenomenon that reaches critical mass and persists for a period of time.
Howard S. Becker	Howard S. Becker is an American sociologist who made major contributions to the sociology of deviance, sociology of art, and sociology of music. Becker also wrote extensively on sociological writing styles and methodologies. In addition, Becker's book The Outsiders provided the foundations for labeling theory. Becker is often called a symbolic interactionist or social constructionist, however he does not align himself with either field. A graduate of the University of Chicago, Becker is considered part of the second Chicago School of Sociology which also includes Erving Goffman, Gary Fine and Anselm Strauss.
Black Power	Black Power is a political slogan and a name for various associated ideologies. It is used in the movement among people of Black African descent throughout the world, though primarily by African Americans in the United States. The movement was prominent in the late 1960s and early 1970s, emphasizing racial pride and the creation of black political and cultural institutions to nurture and promote black collective interests and advance black values.
Labeling theory	Labeling theory is closely related to social-construction and symbolic-interaction analysis. Labeling theory was developed by sociologists during the 1960s. Howard Saul Becker's book Outsiders was extremely influential in the development of this theory and its rise to popularity.
White-collar crime	White-collar crime is a financially motivated, nonviolent crime committed for illegal monetary gain. Within the field of criminology, white-collar crime initially was defined by sociologist Edwin Sutherland in 1939 as 'a crime committed by a person of respectability and high social status in the course of his occupation'. Sutherland was a proponent of symbolic interactionism and believed that criminal behavior was learned from interpersonal interactions.
Primary deviance	Primary deviance is the first stage in a theory of deviant identity formation. Lemert (1967) conceptualized primary deviance as engaging in the initial act of deviance. Primary deviance does not result in a person internalizing a deviant identity, so one does not alter their self-concept to include this deviant identity.
Secondary deviance	Secondary deviance is a stage in a theory of deviant identity formation.

Chapter 6. conformity, Deviance, and Crime

CHAPTER HIGHLIGHTS & NOTES: KEY TERMS, PEOPLE, PLACES, CONCEPTS

Self-fulfilling prophecy	A self-fulfilling prophecy is a prediction that directly or indirectly causes itself to become true, by the very terms of the prophecy itself, due to positive feedback between belief and behavior. Although examples of such prophecies can be found in literature as far back as ancient Greece and ancient India, it is 20th-century sociologist Robert K. Merton who is credited with coining the expression 'self-fulfilling prophecy' and formalizing its structure and consequences. In his book Social Theory and Social Structure, Merton defines self-fulfilling prophecy in the following terms: e.g. when Roxanna falsely believes her marriage will fail, her fears of such failure actually cause the marriage to fail.
National Crime Victimization Survey	The National Crime Victimization Survey administered by the Bureau of Justice Statistics, is a national survey of approximately 49,000 to 77,400 households twice a year in the United States, on the frequency of crime victimization, as well as characteristics and consequences of victimization. The survey focuses on gathering information on the following crimes: assault, burglary, larceny, motor vehicle theft, rape, and robbery. The survey results are used for the purposes of building a crime index.
Property crime	Property crime is a category of crime that includes, among other crimes, burglary, larceny, theft, motor vehicle theft, arson, shoplifting, and vandalism. Property crime only involves the taking of money or property, and does not involve force or threat of force against a victim. Although robbery involves taking property, it is classified as a violent crime, as force or threat of force on an individual that is present is involved in contrast to burglary which is typically of an unoccupied dwelling or other unoccupied building.
Gender crime	A gender crime is a hate crime committed against a specific gender. Specific gender crimes may include some instances of rape, genital mutilation, forced prostitution, and forced pregnancy. Often purported gender crimes are committed during armed conflict or during times of political upheaval or instability.
Crime statistics	Crime statistics attempt to provide statistical measures of the crime in societies. Given that crime is usually secretive by nature, measurements of it are likely to be inaccurate.
	Several methods for measuring crime exist, including household surveys, hospital or insurance records, and compilations by police and similar law enforcement agencies.
Binge drinking	Binge drinking is the modern epithet for drinking alcoholic beverages with the primary intention of becoming intoxicated by heavy consumption of alcohol over a short period of time. It is a kind of purposeful drinking style that is popular in several countries worldwide, and overlaps somewhat with social drinking since it is often done in groups. The degree of intoxication, however, varies between and within various cultures that engage in this practice.

Chapter 6. conformity, Deviance, and Crime

CHAPTER HIGHLIGHTS & NOTES: KEY TERMS, PEOPLE, PLACES, CONCEPTS

Mass murder	Mass murder (in military contexts, sometimes interchangeable with 'mass destruction' or 'genocide') is the act of murdering a large number of people (four or more), typically at the same time or over a relatively short period of time. According to the FBI, mass murder is defined as four or more murders occurring during a particular event with no cooling-off period between the murders. A mass murder typically occurs in a single location in which a number of victims are killed by an individual or more.
Crack cocaine	Crack cocaine is the freebase form of cocaine that can be smoked. It may also be termed rock, hard, iron, cavvy, base, or just crack.

Appearance and characteristics

In purer forms, crack rocks appear as off-white nuggets with jagged edges, with a slightly higher density than candle wax. |
Ecstasy	Ecstasy from the Ancient Greek, ?κ-στασις (ek-stasis), is a subjective experience of total involvement of the subject, with an object of his or her awareness. Total involvement with an object of interest is not an ordinary experience because of being aware of other objects, thus ecstasy is an example of an altered state of consciousness characterized by diminished awareness of other objects or the total lack of the awareness of surroundings and everything around the object. For instance, if one is concentrating on a physical task, then one might cease to be aware of any intellectual thoughts.
Arranged marriage	An arranged marriage is a practice in which someone other than the couple getting married makes the selection of the persons to be wed, meanwhile curtailing or avoiding the process of courtship. Such marriages had deep roots in royal and aristocratic families around the world. Today, arranged marriage is largely practiced in South Asia (India,Nepal, Pakistan, Bangladesh, Sri Lanka), Africa, the Middle East, and Southeast Asia and East Asia to some extent.
Heroin	Heroin (diacetylmorphine or morphine diacetate (INN)), also known as diamorphine (BAN), is an opiate analgesic synthesized by C.R Alder Wright in 1874 by adding two acetyl groups to the molecule morphine, a derivative of the opium poppy. When used in medicine it is typically used to treat severe pain, such as that resulting from a heart attack. It is the 3,6-diacetyl ester of morphine, and functions as a morphine prodrug (meaning that it is metabolically converted to morphine inside the body in order for it to work).
Corporate crime	In criminology, corporate crime refers to crimes committed either by a corporation (i.e., a business entity having a separate legal personality from the natural persons that manage its activities), or by individuals that may be identified with a corporation or other business entity . Note that some forms of corporate corruption may not actually be criminal if they are not specifically illegal under a given system of laws.

Chapter 6. conformity, Deviance, and Crime

CHAPTER HIGHLIGHTS & NOTES: KEY TERMS, PEOPLE, PLACES, CONCEPTS

Organized crime	Organized crime are transnational, national, or local groupings of highly centralized enterprises run by criminals for the purpose of engaging in illegal activity, most commonly for monetary profit. Some criminal organizations, such as terrorist organizations, are politically motivated. Sometimes criminal organizations force people to do business with them, as when a gang extorts money from shopkeepers for 'protection'.
Costs	Costs is a term of art in civil litigation in English law (the law of England and Wales), and in other Commonwealth jurisdictions. After judgment has been given, the judge has the power to order who will pay the lawyers' fees and other disbursements of the parties (the costs). The law of costs defines how such allocation is to take place.
Prison	Prison is a 1988 horror film starring Viggo Mortensen. It was filmed at the Old State Prison in Rawlins, Wyoming with many of its residents on the cast and crew. In 1956, inmate Charlie Forsythe swallowed 60,000 volts of electricity for a murder he did not commit.
Knowledge worker	Knowledge workers are workers whose main capital is knowledge. Typical examples may include software engineers, architects, engineers, scientists and lawyers, because they 'think for a living'. What differentiates knowledge work from other forms of work is its primary task of 'non-routine' problem solving that requires a combination of convergent, divergent, and creative thinking (Reinhardt et al., 2011).
Broken windows theory	The broken windows theory is a criminological theory of the norm setting and signaling effect of urban disorder and vandalism on additional crime and anti-social behavior. The theory states that monitoring and maintaining urban environments in a well-ordered condition may stop further vandalism and escalation into more serious crime Wilson and George L. Kelling.
Community policing	Community policing is a policing strategy and philosophy based on the notion that community interaction and support can help control crime and reduce fear, with community members helping to identify suspects, detain offenders, bring problems to the attention of police, or otherwise target the social problems which give rise to a crime problem in the first place. Community policing is a philosophy that promotes organizational strategies that support the systematic use of partnerships and problem-solving techniques, which proactively address the immediate conditions that give rise to public safety issues such as crime, social disorder, and fear of crime. Community Policing consists of three key components:

Chapter 6. conformity, Deviance, and Crime

CHAPTER HIGHLIGHTS & NOTES: KEY TERMS, PEOPLE, PLACES, CONCEPTS

Target hardening	Target hardening is a term chiefly used by police offices and those working in security, referring to the strengthening of the security of building in order to reduce or minimising the risk of attack or theft. It is believed that a 'strong, visible defense will deter or delay an attack'.
John Braithwaite	John Braithwaite is an academic at the Australian National University (ANU). As a criminologist, he is particularly interested in the role of restorative justice, shame management and reintegration in crime prevention. His book Crime, Shame and Reintegration (1989) demonstrated that current criminal justice practice tends to stigmatize offenders, making the crime problem worse.
Reintegrative shaming	In criminology, the reintegrative shaming theory emphasizes the importance of shame in criminal punishment. The theory holds that punishments should focus on the offender's behavior rather than on the offender. It was developed by Australian criminologist John Braithwaite at Australian National University in 1989.

CHAPTER QUIZ: KEY TERMS, PEOPLE, PLACES, CONCEPTS

1. _____ is an American sociologist who made major contributions to the sociology of deviance, sociology of art, and sociology of music. Becker also wrote extensively on sociological writing styles and methodologies. In addition, Becker's book The Outsiders provided the foundations for labeling theory. Becker is often called a symbolic interactionist or social constructionist, however he does not align himself with either field. A graduate of the University of Chicago, Becker is considered part of the second Chicago School of Sociology which also includes Erving Goffman, Gary Fine and Anselm Strauss.

   a. Howard S. Becker
   b. Electronic discovery
   c. En banc
   d. Equitable tolling

2. . _____ attempt to provide statistical measures of the crime in societies. Given that crime is usually secretive by nature, measurements of it are likely to be inaccurate.

   Several methods for measuring crime exist, including household surveys, hospital or insurance records, and compilations by police and similar law enforcement agencies.

   a. Crime statistics
   b. Gender roles in agriculture
   c. Gendered sexuality

Visit Cram101.com for full Practice Exams

Chapter 6. conformity, Deviance, and Crime

CHAPTER QUIZ: KEY TERMS, PEOPLE, PLACES, CONCEPTS

3. _____ is a stage in a theory of deviant identity formation. Lemert (1967) conceptualized primary deviance as engaging in the initial act of deviance and then posited _____ as the stage in which one internalizes a deviant identity by integrating it into their self-concept.

   a. Secondary deviance
   b. Sexual capital
   c. Showmance
   d. Sign value

4. The _____ administered by the Bureau of Justice Statistics, is a national survey of approximately 49,000 to 77,400 households twice a year in the United States, on the frequency of crime victimization, as well as characteristics and consequences of victimization. The survey focuses on gathering information on the following crimes: assault, burglary, larceny, motor vehicle theft, rape, and robbery. The survey results are used for the purposes of building a crime index.

   a. Visa overstay
   b. National Crime Victimization Survey
   c. Time loop
   d. Two-stage model of free will

5. _____ is a policing strategy and philosophy based on the notion that community interaction and support can help control crime and reduce fear, with community members helping to identify suspects, detain offenders, bring problems to the attention of police, or otherwise target the social problems which give rise to a crime problem in the first place.

   _____ is a philosophy that promotes organizational strategies that support the systematic use of partnerships and problem-solving techniques, which proactively address the immediate conditions that give rise to public safety issues such as crime, social disorder, and fear of crime.

   _____ consists of three key components:

   Community Partnerships: Collaborative partnerships between the law enforcement agency and the individuals and organizations they serve to develop solutions to problems and increase trust in police.

   a. Community policing
   b. Crime science
   c. Defensible Space Theory
   d. Diversion program

Visit Cram101.com for full Practice Exams

ANSWER KEY
Chapter 6. conformity, Deviance, and Crime

1. a
2. a
3. a
4. b
5. a

You can take the complete Chapter Practice Test

for Chapter 6. conformity, Deviance, and Crime
on all key terms, persons, places, and concepts.

Online 99 Cents

http://www.epub4.5.21549.6.cram101.com/

Use www.Cram101.com for all your study needs

including Cram101's online interactive problem solving labs in

chemistry, statistics, mathematics, and more.

Chapter 7. Stratification, Class, and Inequality

CHAPTER OUTLINE: KEY TERMS, PEOPLE, PLACES, CONCEPTS

_____ Social stratification

_____ Caste system

_____ Caste system in India

_____ Endogamy

_____ Life chances

_____ Sex Slaves

_____ Dalit

_____ Kuznets curve

_____ Arranged marriage

_____ Means of production

_____ Capitalism

_____ Surplus value

_____ Kingsley Davis

_____ Social class

_____ Wealth

_____ Occupation

_____ Social status

_____ Upper class

_____ Vanderbilt family

Visit Cram101.com for full Practice Exams

Chapter 7. Stratification, Class, and Inequality

CHAPTER OUTLINE: KEY TERMS, PEOPLE, PLACES, CONCEPTS

_____ Billionaire

_____ Middle class

_____ Millionaire

_____ Upper middle class

_____ Globalization

_____ Lower middle class

_____ Working class

_____ Underclass

_____ Intergenerational mobility

_____ Social mobility

_____ William H. Sewell

_____ War on Poverty

_____ Absolute

_____ Absolute poverty

_____ Poverty threshold

_____ Medicare

_____ Minimum wage

_____ Working poor

_____ Feminization

Visit Cram101.com for full Practice Exams

Chapter 7. Stratification, Class, and Inequality
CHAPTER OUTLINE: KEY TERMS, PEOPLE, PLACES, CONCEPTS

	Feminization of poverty
	Annie E. Casey Foundation
	Social security
	Culture of poverty
	Social exclusion

CHAPTER HIGHLIGHTS & NOTES: KEY TERMS, PEOPLE, PLACES, CONCEPTS

Social stratification	In sociology, social stratification is a concept involving the 'classification of persons into groups based on shared socio-economic conditions ... a relational set of inequalities with economic, social, political and ideological dimensions.' It is a system by which society ranks categories of people in a hierarchy Social stratification is based on four basic principles: (1) Social stratification is a trait of society, not simply a reflection of individual differences; (2) Social stratification carries over from generation to generation; (3) Social stratification is universal but variable; (4) Social stratification involves not just inequality but beliefs as well. In modern Western societies, stratification is broadly organized into three main layers: upper class, middle class, and lower class. Each of these classes can be further subdivided into smaller classes (e.g. occupational).
Caste system	The Caste system in Sri Lanka is a division of society into strata, influenced by the classic Aryan Varnas of North India and the Dravida Jati system found in South India. Ancient Sri Lankan texts such as the Pujavaliya, Sadharmaratnavaliya and Yogaratnakaraya and inscriptional evidence show that the above hierarchy prevailed throughout the feudal period. The repetition of the same caste hierarchy even as recently as the 18th century, in the British / Kandyan period Kadayimpoth - Boundary books as well, indicates the continuation of the tradition right up to the end of Sri Lanka's monarchy.
Caste system in India	The caste system in India is a system of social stratification, social restriction and a basis for affirmative action in India. Historically, the caste system in India defined communities into thousands of endogamous hereditary groups called Jatis.

Chapter 7. Stratification, Class, and Inequality

CHAPTER HIGHLIGHTS & NOTES: KEY TERMS, PEOPLE, PLACES, CONCEPTS

Endogamy	Endogamy is the practice of marrying within a specific ethnic group, class, or social group, rejecting others on such basis as being unsuitable for marriage or other close personal relationships.
	Endogamy is common in many cultures and ethnic groups. Several ethnic religious groups are traditionally more endogamous, although sometimes with the added dimension of requiring marital religious conversion.
Life chances	Life chances is a political theory of the opportunities each individual has to improve his or her quality of life. The concept was introduced by German sociologist Max Weber. It is a probabilistic concept, describing how likely it is, given certain factors, that an individual's life will turn out a certain way.
Sex Slaves	Sex Slaves (also Sex Slave$) is a 2005 documentary by Ric Esther Bienstock which was created in association with CBC, Channel 4 and Canal D. It provides a firsthand account of international human trafficking by going to the countries such as Moldova and Ukraine where girls are recruited, then following the trail to the various countries and locales where they end up. Interviews with traffickers, experts, police vice-squads and former sex slaves, along with undercover footage, provide a glimpse into the frightening reality and scope of the problem.
	One husband's journey is documented as he attempts to rescue his pregnant wife who was sold by a trafficker who befriended them, to a notoriously powerful and violent pimp in Turkey.
Dalit	Dalit, is a self-designation for a group of people traditionally regarded as of Untouchables and unsuitable for making personal relationships. Dalits are a mixed population of numerous caste groups all over South Asia, and speak various languages.
	While the caste system has been abolished under the Indian constitution, there is still discrimination and prejudice against Dalits in South Asia.
Kuznets curve	A Kuznets curve is the graphical representation of Simon Kuznets' hypothesis that as a country develops, there is a natural cycle of economic inequality driven by market forces which at first increases inequality, and then decreases it after a certain average income is attained.
	An example of why this happens is that early in development investment opportunities for those who have money multiply, while wages are held down by an influx of cheap rural labor to the cities. Whereas in mature economies, human capital accrual, or an estimate of cost that has been incurred but not yet paid, takes the place of physical capital accrual as the main source of growth; and inequality slows growth by lowering education levels because poor people lack finance for their education in imperfect credit markets.

Visit Cram101.com for full Practice Exams

Chapter 7. Stratification, Class, and Inequality

CHAPTER HIGHLIGHTS & NOTES: KEY TERMS, PEOPLE, PLACES, CONCEPTS

Arranged marriage	An arranged marriage is a practice in which someone other than the couple getting married makes the selection of the persons to be wed, meanwhile curtailing or avoiding the process of courtship. Such marriages had deep roots in royal and aristocratic families around the world. Today, arranged marriage is largely practiced in South Asia (India,Nepal, Pakistan, Bangladesh, Sri Lanka), Africa, the Middle East, and Southeast Asia and East Asia to some extent.
Means of production	Means of production refers to physical, non-human inputs used in production--the factories, machines, and tools used to produce wealth -- along with both infrastructural capital and natural capital. This includes the classical factors of production minus financial capital and minus human capital. They include two broad categories of objects: instruments of labour (tools, factories, infrastructure, etc).
Capitalism	Capitalism is generally considered to be an economic system that is based on the legal ability to make a return on capital. Some have also used the term as a synonym for competitive markets, wage labor, capital accumulation, voluntary exchange, personal finance and greed. The designation is applied to a variety of historical cases, varying in time, geography, politics, and culture.
Surplus value	Surplus value is a concept used famously by Karl Marx in his critique of political economy. Although Marx did not himself invent the term, he developed the concept. It refers roughly to the new value created by workers in excess of their own labour-cost, a value which Marx said was appropriated by the capitalist as gross profit, and which is the basis of capital accumulation.
Kingsley Davis	Kingsley Davis identified by the American Philosophical Society as one of the most outstanding social scientists of the twentieth century, was a Hoover Institution senior research fellow and internationally recognized American sociologist and demographer. He led and conducted major studies of societies in Europe, South America, Africa and Asia, coined the term 'population explosion,', and played a major role in the naming and development of the demographic transition model. He is also credited with coining the term 'zero population growth' although George Stolnitz claimed to have that distinction.
Social class	Social class is a set of concepts in the social sciences and political theory centered on models of social stratification in which people are grouped into a set of hierarchical social categories. Class is an essential object of analysis for sociologists, political scientists, anthropologists and social historians. However, there is not a consensus on the best definition of the term 'class', and the term has different contextual meanings.
Wealth	Wealth is the abundance of valuable resources or material possessions, or the control of such assets. The word wealth is derived from the old English wela, which is from an Indo-European word stem.

Visit Cram101.com for full Practice Exams

Chapter 7. Stratification, Class, and Inequality

CHAPTER HIGHLIGHTS & NOTES: KEY TERMS, PEOPLE, PLACES, CONCEPTS

Occupation	An as an act of protest, occupation is the entry into and holding of a building, space or symbolic site. As such, occupations often combine some of the following elements: a challenge to ownership of the space involved, an effort to gain public attention, the practical use of the facilities occupied, and a redefinition of the occupied space. Occupations may be conducted with varying degrees of physical force to obtain and defend the place occupied.
Social status	In sociology or anthropology, social status is the honor or prestige attached to one's position in society (one's social position). It may also refer to a rank or position that one holds in a group, for example son or daughter, playmate, pupil, etc. Social status, the position or rank of a person or group within the society, can be determined two ways.
Upper class	The upper class in modern societies is the social class composed of the wealthiest members of society, who also wield the greatest political power. The upper class is generally contained within the wealthiest 1-2% of the population, and is distinguished by immense wealth (in the form of estates) which is passed from generation to generation. The term is often used in conjunction with the terms 'middle class' and 'lower class' as part of a tripartite model of social stratification.
Vanderbilt family	The Vanderbilt family is a significant international family with Dutch origins. Highly prominent during the 19th century due to family patriarch Cornelius Vanderbilt's railroad and shipping empires, the family is known for 'building America's railroads'. Cornelius Vanderbilt's descendants went on to build great Fifth Avenue mansions, Newport, Rhode Island 'summer cottages,' the famous Biltmore House and various other exclusive homes.
Billionaire	A billionaire, in countries that use the short scale number naming system, is a person who has a net worth of at least one billion units of a currency, usually the United States dollar, Euro, or Pound sterling. Forbes magazine updates a complete list of U.S. dollar billionaires around the world every year. There were 1,210 such people in its 2011 list.
Middle class	The middle class is any class of people in the middle of a societal hierarchy. In Weberian socio-economic terms, the middle class is the broad group of people in contemporary society who fall socio-economically between the working class and upper class. The common measures of what constitutes middle class vary significantly between cultures.
Millionaire	A millionaire is an individual whose net worth or wealth is equal to or exceeds one million units of currency. It can also be a person who owns one million units of currency in a bank account or savings account.

Chapter 7. Stratification, Class, and Inequality

CHAPTER HIGHLIGHTS & NOTES: KEY TERMS, PEOPLE, PLACES, CONCEPTS

Upper middle class	The upper middle class is a sociological concept referring to the social group constituted by higher-status members of the middle class. This is in contrast to the term 'lower middle class', which is used for the group at the opposite end of the middle class stratum, and to the broader term 'middle class'. There is considerable debate as to how the upper middle class might be defined.
Globalization	Globalization refers to the increasing global relationships of culture, people, and economic activity. It is generally used to refer to economic globalization: the global distribution of the production of goods and services, through reduction of barriers to international trade such as tariffs, export fees, and import quotas and the reduction of restrictions on the movement of capital and on investment. Globalization may contribute to economic growth in developed and developing countries through increased specialization and the principle of comparative advantage.
Lower middle class	In developed nations across the world, the lower middle class is a sub-division of the greater middle class. Universally the term refers to the group of middle class households or individuals who have not attained the status of the upper middle class associated with the higher realms of the middle class, hence the name. In American society, the middle class may be divided into two or three sub-groups.
Working class	Working class is a term used in the social sciences and in ordinary conversation to describe those employed in lower tier jobs (as measured by skill, education and lower incomes), often extending to those in unemployment or otherwise possessing below-average incomes. Working classes are mainly found in industrialized economies and in urban areas of non-industrialized economies. As with many terms describing social class, working class is defined and used in many different ways.
Underclass	The term underclass is a coinage which functions as a morally neutral equivalent for what was known in the eighteenth and nineteenth centuries as the 'undeserving poor'. The earliest significant exponent of the term was the American sociologist and anthropologist Oscar Lewis in 1961. The underclass, according to Lewis, has 'a strong present-time orientation, with little ability to delay gratification and plan for the future' (p. xxvi).
Intergenerational mobility	Inter-generational mobility refers to the changes in social status and economic mobility which may occur from one generation to another. The concept is applicable to the broad population, as one's economic standing may shift from the position they were born into.

Chapter 7. Stratification, Class, and Inequality

CHAPTER HIGHLIGHTS & NOTES: KEY TERMS, PEOPLE, PLACES, CONCEPTS

Social mobility	Social mobility refers to the movement of individuals or groups in social position over time. It may refer to classes, ethnic groups, or entire nations, and may measure health status, literacy, or education -- but more commonly it refers to individuals or families, and their change in income. It also typically refers to vertical mobility--movement of individuals or groups up from one socio-economic level to another, often by changing jobs or marriage; but can also refer to horizontal mobility--movement from one position to another within the same social level.
William H. Sewell	William Hamilton Sewell (November 27, 1909 - June 24, 2001) was a United States sociologist and the Chancellor of the University of Wisconsin-Madison from 1967-1968. He is known also as the father of another sociologist William H. Sewell, III. William Sewell was born on November 27, 1909, in Perrinton, Michigan. He attended the Michigan State University where he received his BA in 1933 and his MA in 1934, both in sociology. He then attended the University of Minnesota, where he received his PhD in sociology in 1939. He briefly taught at Michigan State and Oklahoma State before he became a professor of sociology at the University of Wisconsin-Madison in 1946, where he stayed until becoming the chancellor in 1967.
War on Poverty	The War on Poverty is the unofficial name for legislation first introduced by United States President Lyndon B. Johnson during his State of the Union address on January 8, 1964. This legislation was proposed by Johnson in response to a national poverty rate of around nineteen percent. The speech led the United States Congress to pass the Economic Opportunity Act, which established the Office of Economic Opportunity (OEO) to administer the local application of federal funds targeted against poverty. As a part of the Great Society, Johnson's belief in expanding the government's role in social welfare programs from education to health care was a continuation of Franklin Delano Roosevelt's New Deal, which ran from 1933 to 1935, and the Four Freedoms of 1941.
Absolute	The Absolute is the concept of an unconditional reality which transcends limited, conditional, everyday existence. It is sometimes used as an alternate term for 'God' or 'the Divine' especially, but by no means exclusively, by those who feel that the term 'God' lends itself too easily to anthropomorphic presumptions. The concept of The Absolute may or may not (depending on one's specific doctrine) possess discrete will, intelligence, awareness or even a personal nature.
Absolute poverty	A measure of absolute poverty quantifies the number of people below a fixed real poverty threshold. It is a level of policy as defined in terms of the minimal requirements necessary to afford minimal standards of food, clothing, health care and shelter. For the measure to be absolute, the line must be the same in different countries, cultures, and technological levels.

Visit Cram101.com for full Practice Exams

Chapter 7. Stratification, Class, and Inequality

CHAPTER HIGHLIGHTS & NOTES: KEY TERMS, PEOPLE, PLACES, CONCEPTS

	Such an absolute measure should look only at the individual's power to consume and it should be independent of any changes in income distribution. Such a measure is possible only when all consumed goods and services are counted and when PPP-exchange rates are used.
Poverty threshold	The poverty threshold, is the minimum level of income deemed adequate in a given country. In practice, like the definition of poverty, the official or common understanding of the poverty line is significantly higher in developed countries than in developing countries. The common international poverty line has in the past been roughly $1 a day.
Medicare	Medicare is a national social insurance program, administered by the U.S. federal government in 1965, that guarantees access to health insurance for Americans ages 65 and older and younger people with disabilities as well as people with end stage renal disease. As a social insurance program, Medicare spreads the financial risk associated with illness across society to protect everyone, and thus has a somewhat different social role from private insurers, which must manage their risk portfolio to guarantee their own solvency. Medicare offers all enrollees a defined benefit.
Minimum wage	A minimum wage is the lowest hourly, daily or monthly remuneration that employers may legally pay to workers. Equivalently, it is the lowest wage at which workers may sell their labour. Although minimum wage laws are in effect in a great many jurisdictions, there are differences of opinion about the benefits and drawbacks of a minimum wage.
Working poor	The working poor are those individuals and families who maintain regular employment but remain in relative poverty due to low levels of pay and dependent expenses. The working poor are often distinguished from paupers, poor who are supported by government aid or charity. Definitions There are various issues to consider when studying the extent, cause and definition of 'working poor' and 'working poor' conditions.
Feminization	In sociology, feminization is the shift in gender roles and sex roles in a society, group, or organization towards a focus upon the feminine. This is the opposite of a cultural focus upon masculinity.

Chapter 7. Stratification, Class, and Inequality

CHAPTER HIGHLIGHTS & NOTES: KEY TERMS, PEOPLE, PLACES, CONCEPTS

Feminization of poverty	The feminization of poverty is a change at levels of poverty biased against women or female-headed households. More specifically, it is an increase in the difference in the levels of poverty among women and men or among female versus male and couple-headed households. It can also mean an increase of the role that gender inequalities have as a determinant of poverty, which would characterize a feminization of the causes of poverty.
Annie E. Casey Foundation	The Annie E. Casey Foundation was started in 1948 in Seattle, Washington, by UPS founder James E. Casey and his siblings George, Harry and Marguerite. It was named in honor of their mother. The foundation moved to Baltimore in 1994.
Social security	Social security is a concept enshrined in Article 22 of the Universal Declaration of Human Rights which states that Everyone, as a member of society, has the right to social security and is entitled to realization, through national effort and international co-operation and in accordance with the organization and resources of each State, of the economic, social and cultural rights indispensable for his dignity and the free development of his personality. In simple term, this means that the signatories agree that society in which a person lives should help them to develop and to make the most of all the advantages (culture, work, social welfare) which are offered to them in the country. Social security may also refer to the action programs of government intended to promote the welfare of the population through assistance measures guaranteeing access to sufficient resources for food and shelter and to promote health and wellbeing for the population at large and potentially vulnerable segments such as children, the elderly, the sick and the unemployed.
Culture of poverty	The culture of poverty is a social theory that expands on the cycle of poverty. Proponents of this theory argue that the poor are not simply lacking resources, but also have a unique value system. According to Oscar Lewis, 'The subculture [of the poor] develops mechanisms that tend to perpetuate it, especially because of what happens to the world view, aspirations, and character of the children who grow up in it.' (Moynihan 1969, p. 199).
Social exclusion	Social exclusion is a concept used in many parts of the world to characterise contemporary forms of social disadvantage. Dr. Lynn Todman, director of the Institute on Social Exclusion at the Adler School of Professional Psychology, suggests that social exclusion refers to processes in which individuals and entire communities of people are systematically blocked from rights, opportunities and resources (e.g. housing, employment, healthcare, civic engagement, democratic participation and due process) that are normally available to members of society and which are key to social integration. The outcome of multiple deprivations that prevent individuals or groups from participating fully in the economic, social, and political life of the society in which they live.

Chapter 7. Stratification, Class, and Inequality

CHAPTER QUIZ: KEY TERMS, PEOPLE, PLACES, CONCEPTS

1. _____, is a self-designation for a group of people traditionally regarded as of Untouchables and unsuitable for making personal relationships. _____s are a mixed population of numerous caste groups all over South Asia, and speak various languages.

    While the caste system has been abolished under the Indian constitution, there is still discrimination and prejudice against _____s in South Asia.

    a. Desegregation
    b. Ethnic cleansing
    c. Hispanophobia
    d. Dalit

2. _____ refers to the increasing global relationships of culture, people, and economic activity. It is generally used to refer to economic _____: the global distribution of the production of goods and services, through reduction of barriers to international trade such as tariffs, export fees, and import quotas and the reduction of restrictions on the movement of capital and on investment. _____ may contribute to economic growth in developed and developing countries through increased specialization and the principle of comparative advantage.

    a. Historical materialism
    b. Globalization
    c. Juglar cycle
    d. Kitchin cycle

3. The _____ is a system of social stratification, social restriction and a basis for affirmative action in India. Historically, the _____ defined communities into thousands of endogamous hereditary groups called Jatis.

    The Jatis were grouped by the Brahminical texts under the four well-known caste categories (the varnas): viz Brahmins, Kshatriyas, Vaishyas, and Shudras.

    a. Cline
    b. Late Glacial Maximum
    c. Paternal mtDNA transmission
    d. Caste system in India

4. . A measure of _____ quantifies the number of people below a fixed real poverty threshold. It is a level of policy as defined in terms of the minimal requirements necessary to afford minimal standards of food, clothing, health care and shelter. For the measure to be absolute, the line must be the same in different countries, cultures, and technological levels. Such an absolute measure should look only at the individual's power to consume and it should be independent of any changes in income distribution. Such a measure is possible only when all consumed goods and services are counted and when PPP-exchange rates are used.

    a. Extended sympathy
    b. Intergenerational equity

Visit Cram101.com for full Practice Exams

Chapter 7. Stratification, Class, and Inequality

CHAPTER QUIZ: KEY TERMS, PEOPLE, PLACES, CONCEPTS

c. Absolute poverty
d. Occupational welfare

5. In sociology, _____ is a concept involving the 'classification of persons into groups based on shared socio-economic conditions ... a relational set of inequalities with economic, social, political and ideological dimensions.' It is a system by which society ranks categories of people in a hierarchy _____ is based on four basic principles: (1) _____ is a trait of society, not simply a reflection of individual differences; (2) _____ carries over from generation to generation; (3) _____ is universal but variable; (4) _____ involves not just inequality but beliefs as well.

In modern Western societies, stratification is broadly organized into three main layers: upper class, middle class, and lower class. Each of these classes can be further subdivided into smaller classes (e.g. occupational).

a. Visa overstay
b. withdrawl
c. Social stratification
d. Cosimo Commisso

ANSWER KEY
Chapter 7. Stratification, Class, and Inequality

1. d
2. b
3. d
4. c
5. c

You can take the complete Chapter Practice Test

for Chapter 7. Stratification, Class, and Inequality
on all key terms, persons, places, and concepts.

Online 99 Cents

http://www.epub4.5.21549.7.cram101.com/

Use www.Cram101.com for all your study needs

including Cram101's online interactive problem solving labs in

chemistry, statistics, mathematics, and more.

Chapter 8. Global Inequality

CHAPTER OUTLINE: KEY TERMS, PEOPLE, PLACES, CONCEPTS

- Wealth
- World Health Organization
- Globalization
- High-income economy
- Lower middle class
- Life expectancy
- Mortality rate
- Population growth
- Infant mortality
- Malnutrition
- Famine
- Confucianism
- Modernization theory
- Karl Marx
- NIE
- Colonialism
- United Students Against Sweatshops
- Sweatshop
- World-system

Visit Cram101.com for full Practice Exams

Chapter 8. Global Inequality

CHAPTER OUTLINE: KEY TERMS, PEOPLE, PLACES, CONCEPTS

	World-systems theory
	Sustainable development
	Economic development

CHAPTER HIGHLIGHTS & NOTES: KEY TERMS, PEOPLE, PLACES, CONCEPTS

Wealth	Wealth is the abundance of valuable resources or material possessions, or the control of such assets. The word wealth is derived from the old English wela, which is from an Indo-European word stem. An individual, community, region or country that possesses an abundance of such possessions or resources is known as wealthy.
World Health Organization	The World Health Organization is a specialized agency of the United Nations (UN) that acts as a coordinating authority on international public health. Established on April 7, 1948, with headquarters in Geneva, Switzerland, the agency inherited the mandate and resources of its predecessor, the Health Organization, which was an agency of the League of Nations. Constitution and history The World Health Organization's constitution states that its objective 'is the attainment by all people of the highest possible level of health.' Its major task is to combat disease, especially key infectious diseases, and to promote the general health of the people of the world.
Globalization	Globalization refers to the increasing global relationships of culture, people, and economic activity. It is generally used to refer to economic globalization: the global distribution of the production of goods and services, through reduction of barriers to international trade such as tariffs, export fees, and import quotas and the reduction of restrictions on the movement of capital and on investment. Globalization may contribute to economic growth in developed and developing countries through increased specialization and the principle of comparative advantage.
High-income economy	A high-income economy is defined by the World Bank as a country with a Gross National Income per capita of $12,196 or more in 2009.

Visit Cram101.com for full Practice Exams

Chapter 8. Global Inequality

CHAPTER HIGHLIGHTS & NOTES: KEY TERMS, PEOPLE, PLACES, CONCEPTS

	While the term 'high income' may be used interchangeably with 'First World' and 'developed country', the technical definitions of these terms differ. The term 'first world' commonly refers to those prosperous countries that aligned themselves with the U.S. and NATO during the cold war. Several institutions, such as the Central Intelligence Agency (CIA) or International Monetary Fund (IMF), take factors other than high per capita income into account when classifying countries as 'developed' or 'advanced economies'.
Lower middle class	In developed nations across the world, the lower middle class is a sub-division of the greater middle class. Universally the term refers to the group of middle class households or individuals who have not attained the status of the upper middle class associated with the higher realms of the middle class, hence the name. In American society, the middle class may be divided into two or three sub-groups.
Life expectancy	Life expectancy is the expected (in the statistical sense) number of years of life remaining at a given age. It is denoted by e_x, which means the average number of subsequent years of life for someone now aged x, according to a particular mortality experience. (In technical literature, this symbol means the average number of complete years of life remaining, excluding fractions of a year.
Mortality rate	Mortality rate is a measure of the number of deaths (in general, or due to a specific cause) in a population, scaled to the size of that population, per unit of time. Mortality rate is typically expressed in units of deaths per 1000 individuals per year; thus, a mortality rate of 9.5 (out of 1000) in a population of 1,000 would mean 9.5 deaths per year in that entire population, or 0.95% out of the total. It is distinct from morbidity rate, which refers to the number of individuals in poor health during a given time period (the prevalence rate) or the number of newly appearing cases of the disease per unit of time (incidence rate).
Population growth	Population growth is the change in a population over time, and can be quantified as the change in the number of individuals of any species in a population using 'per unit time' for measurement In demography, population growth is used informally for the more specific term population growth rate, and is often used to refer specifically to the growth of the human population of the world.
Infant mortality	Infant mortality is defined as the number of infant deaths (one year of age or younger) per 1000 live births. Traditionally, the most common cause worldwide was dehydration from diarrhea.

Chapter 8. Global Inequality

CHAPTER HIGHLIGHTS & NOTES: KEY TERMS, PEOPLE, PLACES, CONCEPTS

Malnutrition	Malnutrition is the condition that results from taking an unbalanced diet in which certain nutrients are lacking, in excess (too high an intake), or in the wrong proportions. A number of different nutrition disorders may arise, depending on which nutrients are under or overabundant in the diet. In most of the world, malnutrition is present in the form of undernutrition, which is caused by a diet lacking adequate calories and protein.
Famine	A famine is a widespread scarcity of food, caused by several factors including crop failure, overpopulation, or government policies. This phenomenon is usually accompanied or followed by regional malnutrition, starvation, epidemic, and increased mortality. Nearly every continent in the world has experienced a period of famine throughout history.
Confucianism	Confucianism is a Chinese ethical and philosophical system developed from the teachings of the Chinese philosopher Confucius (Kong Fuzi, or K'ung-fu-tzu, lit. 'Master Kong', 551-478 BC). It is a complex system of moral, social, political, philosophical, and quasi-religious thought that influenced the culture and history of East Asia.
Modernization theory	Modernization theory is a theory used to explain the process of modernization within societies. The theory looks at the internal factors of a country while assuming that, with assistance, 'traditional' countries can be brought to development in the same manner more developed countries have. Modernization theory attempts to identify the social variables which contribute to social progress and development of societies, and seeks to explain the process of social evolution.
Karl Marx	Karl Heinrich Marx (5 May 1818 - 14 March 1883) was a German philosopher, economist, sociologist, historian, journalist, and revolutionary socialist. His ideas played a significant role in the development of social science and the socialist political movement. He published various books during his lifetime, with the most notable being The Communist Manifesto (1848) and Capital (1867-1894); some of his works were co-written with his friend, the fellow German revolutionary socialist Friedrich Engels. Born into a wealthy middle class family in Trier, formerly in Prussian Rhineland now called Rhineland-Palatinate, Marx studied at both the University of Bonn and the University of Berlin, where he became interested in the philosophical ideas of the Young Hegelians. In 1836, he became engaged to Jenny von Westphalen, marrying her in 1843. After his studies, he wrote for a radical newspaper in Cologne, and began to work out his theory of dialectical materialism. Moving to Paris in 1843, he began writing for other radical newspapers. He met Engels in Paris, and the two men worked together on a series of books. Exiled to Brussels, he became a leading figure of the Communist League, before moving back to Cologne, where he founded his own newspaper. In 1849 he was exiled again and moved to London together with his wife and children.

Chapter 8. Global Inequality

CHAPTER HIGHLIGHTS & NOTES: KEY TERMS, PEOPLE, PLACES, CONCEPTS

In London, where the family was reduced to poverty, Marx continued writing and formulating his theories about the nature of society and how he believed it could be improved, as well as campaigning for socialism and becoming a significant figure in the International Workingmen's Association.

Marx's theories about society, economics and politics, which are collectively known as Marxism, hold that all societies progress through the dialectic of class struggle; a conflict between an ownership class which controls production and a lower class which produces the labour for such goods. Heavily critical of the current socio-economic form of society, capitalism, he called it the 'dictatorship of the bourgeoisie', believing it to be run by the wealthy classes purely for their own benefit, and predicted that, like previous socioeconomic systems, it would inevitably produce internal tensions which would lead to its self-destruction and replacement by a new system, socialism. He argued that under socialism society would be governed by the working class in what he called the 'dictatorship of the proletariat', the 'workers state' or 'workers' democracy'. He believed that socialism would, in its turn, eventually be replaced by a stateless, classless society called communism. Along with believing in the inevitability of socialism and communism, Marx actively fought for the former's implementation, arguing that both social theorists and underprivileged people should carry out organised revolutionary action to topple capitalism and bring about socio-economic change.

Revolutionary socialist governments espousing Marxist concepts took power in a variety of countries in the 20th century, leading to the formation of such socialist states as the Soviet Union in 1922 and the People's Republic of China in 1949, while various theoretical variants, such as Leninism, Stalinism, Trotskyism and Maoism, were developed. Marx is typically cited, with Émile Durkheim and Max Weber, as one of the three principal architects of modern social science. Marx has been described as one of the most influential figures in human history, and in a 1999 BBC poll was voted the top 'thinker of the millennium' by people from around the world. Biography Early life: 1818-1835

Karl Heinrich Marx was born on 5 May 1818 at 664 Brückergasse in Trier, a town located in the Kingdom of Prussia's Province of the Lower Rhine. His ancestry was Jewish, with his paternal line having supplied the rabbis of Trier since 1723, a role that had been taken up by his own grandfather, Meier Halevi Marx; Meier's son and Karl's father would be the first in the line to receive a secular education. His maternal grandfather was a Dutch rabbi. Karl's father, Herschel Marx, was middle-class and relatively wealthy: the family owned a number of Moselle vineyards; he converted from Judaism to the Protestant Christian denomination of Lutheranism prior to his son's birth, taking on the German forename of Heinrich over Herschel. In 1815, he began working as an attorney and in 1819 moved his family from a five-room rented apartment into a ten-room property near the Porta Nigra. A man of the Enlightenment, Heinrich Marx was interested in the ideas of the philosophers Immanuel Kant and Voltaire, and took part in agitation for a constitution and reforms in Prussia, which was then governed by an absolute monarchy.

Chapter 8. Global Inequality

CHAPTER HIGHLIGHTS & NOTES: KEY TERMS, PEOPLE, PLACES, CONCEPTS

	Karl's mother, born Henrietta Pressburg, was a Dutch Jew who, unlike her husband, was only semi-literate. She claimed to suffer from 'excessive mother love', devoting much time to her family, and insisting on cleanliness within her home. She was from a prosperous business family. Her family later founded the company Philips Electronics: she was great-aunt to Anton and Gerard Philips, and great-great-aunt to Frits Philips. Her brother, Marx's uncle Benjamin Philips (1830-1900), was a wealthy banker and industrialist, who Karl and Jenny Marx would later often come rely upon for loans, while they were exiled in London. Little is known about Karl Marx's childhood.
NIE	NIE, short for Niepodleglosc ('Independence'), 'NIE' means also 'NO' in Polish - was a Polish anticommunist resistance organisation formed in 1943 in a case of a Soviet occupation of Poland. Its main goal was the struggle against the Soviet Union after 1944. NIE was one of the most well hidden structures of Armia Krajowa, active to 7 May 1945. Its commanders were General Leopold Okulicki and Emil August Fieldorf. One of the first members of the organisation was Witold Pilecki.
Colonialism	Colonialism is the establishment, maintenance, acquisition and expansion of colonies in one territory by people from another territory. It is a process whereby the metropole claims sovereignty over the colony, and the social structure, government, and economics of the colony are changed by colonizers from the metropole. Colonialism is a set of unequal relationships between the metropole and the colony and between the colonists and the indigenous population.
United Students Against Sweatshops	United Students Against Sweatshops is a student organization with chapters at over 250 colleges and universities in the United States and Canada. In April 2000, USAS founded the Worker Rights Consortium (WRC), an independent monitoring organization that investigates labor conditions in factories that produce collegiate apparel all over the world. The WRC exacts an annual membership fee from participating universities, which is used to fund its monitoring work.
Sweatshop	Sweatshop is a negatively connoted term for any working environment considered to be unacceptably difficult or dangerous. Sweatshop workers often work long hours for very low pay, regardless of laws mandating overtime pay or a minimum wage. Child labour laws may be violated.
World-system	World-system is a crucial element of the world-system theory, a multidisciplinary, macro-scale approach to world history and social change. Within that theory, world-system means a socioeconomic system, one encompassing part of or the entirety of the globe. World-systems are usually larger than single countries (nations), but do not have to be global.

Chapter 8. Global Inequality

CHAPTER HIGHLIGHTS & NOTES: KEY TERMS, PEOPLE, PLACES, CONCEPTS

World-systems theory	World-systems theory is a multidisciplinary, macro-scale approach to world history and social change. World-systems theory stresses that the world-system (and not nation states) should be the basic unit of social analysis. World-system refers to the international division of labor, which divides the world into core countries, semi-periphery countries and the periphery countries.
Sustainable development	Sustainable development is a pattern of economic growth in which resource use aims to meet human needs while preserving the environment so that these needs can be met not only in the present, but also for generations to come (sometimes taught as ELF-Environment, Local people, Future). The term 'sustainable development' was used by the Brundtland Commission which coined what has become the most often-quoted definition of sustainable development as development that 'meets the needs of the present without compromising the ability of future generations to meet their own needs.' Alternatively, sustainability educator Michael Thomas Needham referred to 'Sustainable Development' 'as the ability to meet the needs of the present while contributing to the future generations' needs.' There is an additional focus on the present generations responsibility to improve the future generations life by restoring the previous ecosystem damage and resisting to contribute to further ecosystem damage. Sustainable development ties together concern for the carrying capacity of natural systems with the social challenges faced by humanity.
Economic development	Economic development generally refers to the sustained, concerted actions of policymakers and communities that promote the standard of living and economic health of a specific area. Economic development can also be referred to as the quantitative and qualitative changes in the economy. Such actions can involve multiple areas including development of human capital, critical infrastructure, regional competitiveness, environmental sustainability, social inclusion, health, safety, literacy, and other initiatives.

Chapter 8. Global Inequality

CHAPTER QUIZ: KEY TERMS, PEOPLE, PLACES, CONCEPTS

1. In developed nations across the world, the _____ is a sub-division of the greater middle class. Universally the term refers to the group of middle class households or individuals who have not attained the status of the upper middle class associated with the higher realms of the middle class, hence the name.

   In American society, the middle class may be divided into two or three sub-groups.

   a. Maya social classes
   b. Lower middle class
   c. Professional-managerial class
   d. Ruling class

2. The _____ is a specialized agency of the United Nations (UN) that acts as a coordinating authority on international public health. Established on April 7, 1948, with headquarters in Geneva, Switzerland, the agency inherited the mandate and resources of its predecessor, the Health Organization, which was an agency of the League of Nations.

   Constitution and history

   The _____'s constitution states that its objective 'is the attainment by all people of the highest possible level of health.' Its major task is to combat disease, especially key infectious diseases, and to promote the general health of the people of the world.

   a. World Health Report
   b. 1918 flu pandemic
   c. Visa overstay
   d. World Health Organization

3. _____ is the abundance of valuable resources or material possessions, or the control of such assets. The word _____ is derived from the old English wela, which is from an Indo-European word stem. An individual, community, region or country that possesses an abundance of such possessions or resources is known as wealthy.

   a. Welfare cost of inflation
   b. Wealth
   c. Benefitive treasury measure
   d. Bodily integrity

4. A _____ is defined by the World Bank as a country with a Gross National Income per capita of $12,196 or more in 2009. While the term 'high income' may be used interchangeably with 'First World' and 'developed country', the technical definitions of these terms differ. The term 'first world' commonly refers to those prosperous countries that aligned themselves with the U.S. and NATO during the cold war. Several institutions, such as the Central Intelligence Agency (CIA) or International Monetary Fund (IMF), take factors other than high per capita income into account when classifying countries as 'developed' or 'advanced economies'.

   a. Third World

Visit Cram101.com for full Practice Exams

Chapter 8. Global Inequality

CHAPTER QUIZ: KEY TERMS, PEOPLE, PLACES, CONCEPTS

   b. Balkanization
   c. Politics of Kanagawa
   d. High-income economy

5. _____ refers to the increasing global relationships of culture, people, and economic activity. It is generally used to refer to economic _____: the global distribution of the production of goods and services, through reduction of barriers to international trade such as tariffs, export fees, and import quotas and the reduction of restrictions on the movement of capital and on investment. _____ may contribute to economic growth in developed and developing countries through increased specialization and the principle of comparative advantage.

   a. Historical materialism
   b. Human evolution
   c. Globalization
   d. Kitchin cycle

ANSWER KEY
Chapter 8. Global Inequality

1. b
2. d
3. b
4. d
5. c

You can take the complete Chapter Practice Test

for Chapter 8. Global Inequality
on all key terms, persons, places, and concepts.

Online 99 Cents

http://www.epub4.5.21549.8.cram101.com/

Use www.Cram101.com for all your study needs

including Cram101's online interactive problem solving labs in

chemistry, statistics, mathematics, and more.

Chapter 9. Gender Inequality

CHAPTER OUTLINE: KEY TERMS, PEOPLE, PLACES, CONCEPTS

- Gender inequality
- Testosterone
- Bacha posh
- Patriarchy
- Sex segregation
- Glass ceiling
- Economic inequality
- Women in the workforce
- Child care
- Occupation
- Sexual harassment
- Prostitution
- Violence against women
- Functionalism
- Liberal feminism
- National Women's Conference
- Radical feminism
- Apartheid
- Women's liberation movement

Visit Cram101.com for full Practice Exams

Chapter 9. Gender Inequality
CHAPTER OUTLINE: KEY TERMS, PEOPLE, PLACES, CONCEPTS

- Black feminism
- Suffragette

CHAPTER HIGHLIGHTS & NOTES: KEY TERMS, PEOPLE, PLACES, CONCEPTS

Gender inequality	Gender inequality refers to disparity between individuals due to gender. Gender is constructed both socially through social interactions as well as biologically through chromosomes, brain structure, and hormonal differences. Gender systems are often dichotomous and hierarchical; binary gender systems may reflect the inequalities that manifest in numerous dimensions of daily life.
Testosterone	Testosterone is a steroid hormone from the androgen group and is found in mammals, reptiles, birds, and other vertebrates. In mammals, testosterone is primarily secreted in the testicles of males and the ovaries of females, although small amounts are also secreted by the adrenal glands. It is the principal male sex hormone and an anabolic steroid.
Bacha posh	Bacha posh is a cultural practice in areas of Afghanistan where a family in which there are no sons may have a girl dress in characteristic male clothing and have her hair cut short, occupying an intermediate status in which she is treated as neither a daughter nor fully as a son. In Afghan culture, pressure exists to have a son to carry on the family name and to inherit his father's property. In the absence of a son, families may dress one of their daughters as a male, with some holding the superstition that having a bacha posh will make it more likely for a woman to give birth to a son in a subsequent pregnancy.
Patriarchy	Patriarchy is a social system in which the role of the male as the primary authority figure is central to social organization, and where fathers hold authority over women, children, and property. It implies the institutions of male rule and privilege, and is dependent on female subordination. Historically, patriarchy has manifested itself in the social, legal, political, and economic organization of a range of different cultures, and also influences modern civilization.
Sex segregation	Sex segregation is the separation of people according to their sex.

Chapter 9. Gender Inequality

CHAPTER HIGHLIGHTS & NOTES: KEY TERMS, PEOPLE, PLACES, CONCEPTS

	The term gender apartheid also has been applied to segregation of people by gender, implying that it is sexual discrimination. In some circumstances, gender segregation is a controversial policy, with critics contending that in most or all circumstances it is a violation of human rights, and supporters arguing that it is necessary to maintain decency, sacredness, modesty, female safety, or the family unit.
Glass ceiling	In economics, the term glass ceiling refers to 'the unseen, yet unbreachable barrier that keeps minorities and women from rising to the upper rungs of the corporate ladder, regardless of their qualifications or achievements.' Initially, the metaphor applied to barriers in the careers of women but was quickly extended to refer to obstacles hindering the advancement of minority men, as well as women.

David Cotter et al. defined four distinctive characteristics that must be met to conclude that a glass ceiling exists. A glass ceiling inequality represents:•'A gender or racial difference that is not explained by other job-relevant characteristics of the employee.'•'A gender or racial difference that is greater at higher levels of an outcome than at lower levels of an outcome.•'A gender or racial inequality in the chances of advancement into higher levels, not merely the proportions of each gender or race currently at those higher levels.'•'A gender or racial inequality that increases over the course of a career.'

Cotter and his colleagues found that glass ceilings are a distinctively gender phenomenon. |
Economic inequality	Economic inequality comprises disparities in the distribution of economic assets (wealth) and income within or between populations or individuals. The term typically refers to inequality among individuals and groups within a society, but can also refer to inequality among countries. The issue of economic inequality is related to the ideas of equity, equality of outcome and equality of opportunity.
Women in the workforce	Women in the workforce earning wages or a salary are part of a modern phenomenon, one that developed at the same time as the growth of paid employment for men; yet women have been challenged by inequality in the workforce. Until modern times, legal and cultural practices, combined with the inertia of longstanding religious and educational conventions, restricted women's entry and participation in the workforce. Economic dependency upon men, and consequently the poor socio-economic status of women, have had the same impact, particularly as occupations have become professionalized over the 19th and 20th centuries.
Child care	Child care means caring for and supervising a child or children, usually from newborn to age thirteen. Child care is the action or skill of looking after children by a day-care center, babysitter, or other providers.

Chapter 9. Gender Inequality

CHAPTER HIGHLIGHTS & NOTES: KEY TERMS, PEOPLE, PLACES, CONCEPTS

Occupation	An as an act of protest, occupation is the entry into and holding of a building, space or symbolic site. As such, occupations often combine some of the following elements: a challenge to ownership of the space involved, an effort to gain public attention, the practical use of the facilities occupied, and a redefinition of the occupied space. Occupations may be conducted with varying degrees of physical force to obtain and defend the place occupied.
Sexual harassment	Sexual harassment is intimidation, bullying or coercion of a sexual nature, or the unwelcome or inappropriate promise of rewards in exchange for sexual favors. In most modern legal contexts sexual harassment is illegal. As defined by EEOC, 'It is unlawful to harass a person (an applicant or employee) because of that person's sex.' Harassment can include 'sexual harassment' or unwelcome sexual advances, requests for sexual favors, and other verbal or physical harassment of a sexual nature.
Prostitution	Prostitution is the act or practice of providing sexual services to another person in return for payment. People who execute such activities are called prostitutes. Prostitution is one of the branches of the sex industry.
Violence against women	Violence against women is a technical term used to collectively refer to violent acts that are primarily or exclusively committed against women. Similar to a hate crime, this type of violence targets a specific group with the victim's gender as a primary motive. The United Nations General Assembly defines 'violence against women' as 'any act of gender-based violence that results in, or is likely to result in, physical, sexual or mental harm or suffering to women, including threats of such acts, coercion or arbitrary deprivation of liberty, whether occurring in public or in private life.' The 1993 Declaration on the Elimination of Violence Against Women noted that this violence could be perpetrated by assailants of either gender, family members and even the 'State' itself.
Functionalism	Functionalism is a theory of the mind in contemporary philosophy, developed largely as an alternative to both the identity theory of mind and behaviourism. Its core idea is that mental states (beliefs, desires, being in pain, etc). are constituted solely by their functional role -- that is, they are causal relations to other mental states, sensory inputs, and behavioral outputs.
Liberal feminism	Liberal feminism is an individualistic form of feminism theory, which primarily focuses on women's ability to show and maintain their equality through their own actions and choices. Liberal feminists argue that our society holds the false belief that women are, by nature, less intellectually and physically capable than men, it tends to discriminate against women in the academy, the forum, and the marketplace. Liberal feminists believe that 'female subordination is rooted in a set of customary and legal constraints that blocks women's entrance to and success in the so-called public world' and they work hard to emphasize the equality of men and women through political and legal reform.

Chapter 9. Gender Inequality

CHAPTER HIGHLIGHTS & NOTES: KEY TERMS, PEOPLE, PLACES, CONCEPTS

National Women's Conference	In the spirit of the United Nations' proclamation that 1975 was the International Women's Year, on January 9, 1974, U.S. President Gerald Ford issued Executive Order 11832 creating a National Commission on the Observance of International Women's Year 'to promote equality between men and women'. In 1977 President Jimmy Carter chose a new Commission and appointed Congresswoman Bella Abzug to head it. Numerous events were held over the next two years, culminating in the National Women's Conference in November 1977. Event During November 18-21, 1977, twenty-thousand women descended upon Houston, Texas for the National Women's Conference.
Radical feminism	Radical feminism is a current theoretical perspective within feminism that focuses on the theory of patriarchy as a system of power that organizes society into a complex of relationships based on an assumption that male supremacy oppresses women. Radical feminism aims to challenge and overthrow patriarchy by opposing standard gender roles and oppression of women and calls for a radical reordering of society. Early radical feminism, arising within second-wave feminism in the 1960s, typically viewed patriarchy as a 'transhistorical phenomenon' prior to or deeper than other sources of oppression, 'not only the oldest and most universal form of domination but the primary form' and the model for all others.
Apartheid	Apartheid is an Afrikaans word for a system of racial segregation enforced through legislation by the National Party governments, who were the ruling party from 1948 to 1994, of South Africa, under which the rights of the majority black inhabitants of South Africa were curtailed and white supremacy and Afrikaner minority rule was maintained. Literally translated it means 'the status of being apart'. Apartheid was developed after World War II by the Afrikaner-dominated National Party and Broederbond organizations and was practiced also in South West Africa, which was administered by South Africa under a League of Nations mandate (revoked in 1966 via United Nations Resolution 2145), until it gained independence as Namibia in 1990.
Women's liberation movement	The women's liberation movement should not be taken to be synonymous with feminism: the women's liberation movement, was a feminist movement, but not all feminists have been in the Women's liberation movement. This is because it was a specific historical movement. It generated mythology almost before it was born such as bra burning - and it was allegedly a matter of deep concern to those within it at the time that its history would allegedly be rewritten by those who weren't in it. Allegedly one important reality was that it is more sensibly seen as a movement of the 1970s and 1980s, not the 1960s, despite allegedly often being described as a 1960s phenomenon.

Chapter 9. Gender Inequality

CHAPTER HIGHLIGHTS & NOTES: KEY TERMS, PEOPLE, PLACES, CONCEPTS

Black feminism	Black Feminism argues that sexism, class oppression, and racism are inextricably bound together. Forms of feminism that strive to overcome sexism and class oppression. The Combahee River Collective argued in 1974 that the liberation of black women entails freedom for all people, since it would require the end of racism, sexism, and class oppression.
Suffragette	Suffragette is a term originally coined by the Daily Mail newspaper as a derogatory label for members of the late-19th and early-20th century movement for women's suffrage in the United Kingdom, in particular members of the Women's Social and Political Union (WSPU). However, after former and then active members of the movement began to reclaim the word, the term became a label without negative connotations. They wanted to be involved in the running of the country and they wanted to be treated as equals to men.

CHAPTER QUIZ: KEY TERMS, PEOPLE, PLACES, CONCEPTS

1. _____ is a term originally coined by the Daily Mail newspaper as a derogatory label for members of the late-19th and early-20th century movement for women's suffrage in the United Kingdom, in particular members of the Women's Social and Political Union (WSPU). However, after former and then active members of the movement began to reclaim the word, the term became a label without negative connotations. They wanted to be involved in the running of the country and they wanted to be treated as equals to men.

    a. Swedish Society for Woman Suffrage
    b. The Second Stage
    c. Theodora
    d. Suffragette

2. _____ is a cultural practice in areas of Afghanistan where a family in which there are no sons may have a girl dress in characteristic male clothing and have her hair cut short, occupying an intermediate status in which she is treated as neither a daughter nor fully as a son. In Afghan culture, pressure exists to have a son to carry on the family name and to inherit his father's property. In the absence of a son, families may dress one of their daughters as a male, with some holding the superstition that having a _____ will make it more likely for a woman to give birth to a son in a subsequent pregnancy.

    a. Bahuchara Mata
    b. Bissu
    c. Bugis Street
    d. Bacha posh

3. . An as an act of protest, _____ is the entry into and holding of a building, space or symbolic site.

Chapter 9. Gender Inequality

CHAPTER QUIZ: KEY TERMS, PEOPLE, PLACES, CONCEPTS

As such, _____s often combine some of the following elements: a challenge to ownership of the space involved, an effort to gain public attention, the practical use of the facilities occupied, and a redefinition of the occupied space. _____s may be conducted with varying degrees of physical force to obtain and defend the place occupied.

a. Occupy movement
b. Open rescue
c. Operation Lincoln
d. Occupation

4. _____ refers to disparity between individuals due to gender. Gender is constructed both socially through social interactions as well as biologically through chromosomes, brain structure, and hormonal differences. Gender systems are often dichotomous and hierarchical; binary gender systems may reflect the inequalities that manifest in numerous dimensions of daily life.

a. Gender inequality
b. Housing inequality
c. Hypergamy
d. Kyriarchy

5. _____ is a steroid hormone from the androgen group and is found in mammals, reptiles, birds, and other vertebrates. In mammals, _____ is primarily secreted in the testicles of males and the ovaries of females, although small amounts are also secreted by the adrenal glands. It is the principal male sex hormone and an anabolic steroid.

a. Testosterone
b. Housing inequality
c. Hypergamy
d. Kyriarchy

ANSWER KEY
Chapter 9. Gender Inequality

1. d
2. d
3. d
4. a
5. a

You can take the complete Chapter Practice Test

for Chapter 9. Gender Inequality
on all key terms, persons, places, and concepts.

Online 99 Cents

http://www.epub4.5.21549.9.cram101.com/

Use www.Cram101.com for all your study needs

including Cram101's online interactive problem solving labs in

chemistry, statistics, mathematics, and more.

Chapter 10. Ethnicity and Race

CHAPTER OUTLINE: KEY TERMS, PEOPLE, PLACES, CONCEPTS

- Racialization
- Racism
- Scientific racism
- Displacement
- Dominant group
- Scapegoating
- Melting pot
- Genocide
- Holocaust
- Ku Klux Klan
- Armenian Genocide
- Loving v. Virginia
- Serbs
- Apartheid
- Assimilation
- Multiculturalism
- Pluralism
- Emigration
- Ethnic group

Visit Cram101.com for full Practice Exams

Chapter 10. Ethnicity and Race

CHAPTER OUTLINE: KEY TERMS, PEOPLE, PLACES, CONCEPTS

- Diaspora
- Bogardus social distance scale
- Emory S. Bogardus
- Chinese Exclusion Act
- Globalization
- Black Codes
- Rosa Parks
- Civil rights movement
- Cultural group
- Wealth
- Residential segregation
- Ghetto
- Political power
- William Julius Wilson

Visit Cram101.com for full Practice Exams

Chapter 10. Ethnicity and Race

CHAPTER HIGHLIGHTS & NOTES: KEY TERMS, PEOPLE, PLACES, CONCEPTS

Racialization	Racialization refers to processes of the discursive production of racial identities. It signifies the extension of dehumanizing and racial meanings to a previously racially unclassified relationship, social practice, or group. Put simply, a group of people is seen as a 'race', when it was not before.
Racism	Racism is the belief that the genetic factors which constitute race, ethnicity, or nationality are a primary determinant of human traits and capacities and that ethnic differences produce an inherent superiority of a particular race. Racism's effects are called 'racial discrimination.' In the case of institutional racism, certain racial groups may be denied rights or benefits, or receive preferential treatment. Racial discrimination typically points out taxonomic differences between different groups of people, although anyone may be discriminated against on an ethnic or cultural basis, independently of their somatic differences.
Scientific racism	Scientific racism is the use of scientific techniques and hypotheses to sanction the belief in racial superiority, inferiority or racism. This is not the same as using scientific findings and the scientific method to investigate differences among races. In biological classification differences between animal groups are investigated without necessarily claiming that one group is superior to others.
Displacement	In Freudian psychology, displacement is an unconscious defense mechanism whereby the mind redirects effects from an object felt to be dangerous or unacceptable to an object felt to be safe or acceptable. The term originated with Sigmund Freud. Displacement operates in the mind unconsciously and involves emotions, ideas, or wishes being transferred from their original object to a more acceptable substitute.
Dominant group	A dominant group is the group whose interests a system is meant to serve and whose identity it is meant to represent. The system is a form of government where representatives of a particular group hold a number of posts disproportionately large to the percentage of the total population that the particular group represents and uses them to advance the position of their particular group to the detriment of others. A group is dominant if it possesses a disproportionate share of societal resources, privileges, and power.
Scapegoating	Scapegoating is the practice of singling out any party for unmerited negative treatment or blame as a scapegoat.

Chapter 10. Ethnicity and Race

CHAPTER HIGHLIGHTS & NOTES: KEY TERMS, PEOPLE, PLACES, CONCEPTS

	Scapegoating may be conducted by individuals against individuals (e.g., 'Jimmy did it, not me!'), individuals against groups (e.g., 'I failed because our school favors boys'), groups against individuals (e.g., 'Jane was the reason our team didn't win'), and groups against groups (e.g., 'Immigrants are taking all of the jobs').
	A scapegoat may be an adult, sibling, child, employee, peer, ethnic or religious group, or country.
Melting pot	The melting pot is a metaphor for a heterogeneous society becoming more homogeneous, the different elements 'melting together' into a harmonious whole with a common culture. It is particularly used to describe the assimilation of immigrants to the United States; the melting-together metaphor was in use by the 1780s.
	After 1970 the desirability of assimilation and the melting pot model was challenged by proponents of multiculturalism, who assert that cultural differences within society are valuable and should be preserved, proposing the alternative metaphor of the mosaic or salad bowl - different cultures mix, but remain distinct.
Genocide	Genocide is the deliberate and systematic destruction, in whole or in part, of an ethnic, racial, religious, or national group. While a precise definition varies among genocide scholars, a legal definition is found in the 1948 United Nations Convention on the Prevention and Punishment of the Crime of Genocide'
	The preamble to the CPPCG states that instances of genocide have taken place throughout history, but it was not until Raphael Lemkin coined the term and the prosecution of perpetrators of the Holocaust at the Nuremberg trials that the United Nations agreed to the CPPCG which defined the crime of genocide under international law.
Holocaust	The Holocaust also known as the Shoah, was the mass murder or genocide of approximately six million Jews during World War II, a programme of systematic state-sponsored murder by Nazi Germany, led by Adolf Hitler and the Nazi Party, throughout German-occupied territory. Of the nine million Jews who had resided in Europe before the Holocaust, approximately two-thirds were killed. Over one million Jewish children were killed in the Holocaust, as were approximately two million Jewish women and three million Jewish men.
Ku Klux Klan	Ku Klux Klan, often abbreviated Ku Klux Klan and informally known as The Klan, is the name of three distinct past and present far-right organizations in the United States, which have advocated extremist reactionary currents such as white supremacy, white nationalism, and anti-immigration, historically expressed through terrorism. Since the mid-20th century, the Ku Klux Klan has also been anti-communist. The current manifestation is splintered into several chapters and is classified as a hate group.

Visit Cram101.com for full Practice Exams

Chapter 10. Ethnicity and Race

CHAPTER HIGHLIGHTS & NOTES: KEY TERMS, PEOPLE, PLACES, CONCEPTS

Armenian Genocide	The Armenian Genocide was the systematic killing of the Armenian population of the Ottoman Empire during and just after World War I. It was implemented through wholesale massacres and deportations, with the deportations consisting of forced marches under conditions designed to lead to the death of the deportees. The total number of resulting Armenian deaths is generally held to have been between 1 million and 1.5 million. Other ethnic groups were similarly attacked by the Ottoman Empire during this period, including Assyrians and Greeks, and some scholars consider those events to be part of the same policy of extermination.
Loving v. Virginia	Loving v. Virginia, 388 U.S. 1 (1967), was a landmark civil rights case in which the United States Supreme Court, by a 9-0 vote, declared Virginia's anti-miscegenation statute, the 'Racial Integrity Act of 1924', unconstitutional, thereby overturning Pace v. Alabama (1883) and ending all race-based legal restrictions on marriage in the United States.

Facts

The plaintiffs, Mildred Loving (née Mildred Delores Jeter, a woman of African and Rappahannock Native American descent, July 22, 1939 - May 2, 2008) and Richard Perry Loving (a white man, October 29, 1933 - June 1975), were residents of the Commonwealth of Virginia who had been married in June 1958 in the District of Columbia, having left Virginia to evade the Racial Integrity Act, a state law banning marriages between any white person and any non-white person. Upon their return to Caroline County, Virginia, they were charged with violation of the ban. |
Serbs	Serbs are a South Slavic ethnic group of the Balkans. Serbs are located mainly in Serbia, Montenegro and Bosnia and Herzegovina, and are also a significant minority in other republics of the former Yugoslavia- primarily Croatia, the Republic of Macedonia and Slovenia. Likewise, Serbs are an officially recognized minority in both Romania and Hungary, as well as Albania and Slovakia.
Apartheid	Apartheid is an Afrikaans word for a system of racial segregation enforced through legislation by the National Party governments, who were the ruling party from 1948 to 1994, of South Africa, under which the rights of the majority black inhabitants of South Africa were curtailed and white supremacy and Afrikaner minority rule was maintained. Literally translated it means 'the status of being apart'. Apartheid was developed after World War II by the Afrikaner-dominated National Party and Broederbond organizations and was practiced also in South West Africa, which was administered by South Africa under a League of Nations mandate (revoked in 1966 via United Nations Resolution 2145), until it gained independence as Namibia in 1990.
Assimilation	Cultural assimilation is a socio-political response to demographic multi-ethnicity that supports or promotes the assimilation of ethnic minorities into the dominant culture. It is opposed to affirmative philosophy (for example, multiculturalism) which recognizes and works to maintain differences.

Chapter 10. Ethnicity and Race

CHAPTER HIGHLIGHTS & NOTES: KEY TERMS, PEOPLE, PLACES, CONCEPTS

Multiculturalism	Multiculturalism is an ideology that promotes the institutionalisation of communities containing multiple cultures. It is generally applied to the demographic make-up of a specific place, usually at the organizational level, e.g. schools, businesses, neighbourhoods, cities, or nations. In a political context the term is used for a wide variety of meanings, ranging from the advocacy of equal respect to the various cultures in a society, to a policy of promoting the maintenance of cultural diversity, to policies in which people of various ethnic and religious groups are addressed by the authorities as defined by the group they belong to.
Pluralism	Classical pluralism is the view that politics and decision making are located mostly in the framework of government, but that many non-governmental groups use their resources to exert influence. The central question for classical pluralism is how power and influence is distributed in a political process. Groups of individuals try to maximize their interests.
Emigration	Emigration is the act of leaving one's country or region to settle in another. It is the same as immigration but from the perspective of the country of origin. Human movement in general is termed migration.
Ethnic group	An ethnic group is a group of people whose members are identified through a common trait. This can, but does not have to, include an idea of common heritage, a common culture, a shared language or dialect. The group's ethos or ideology may also stress common ancestry and religion, as opposed to an ethnic minority group which refers to race.
Diaspora	Diaspora (stylized DIASPORA*) is a free personal web server that implements a distributed social networking service. Installations of the software form nodes (termed 'pods') which make up the distributed Diaspora social network. The project was founded by Dan Grippi, Maxwell Salzberg, Raphael Sofaer and Ilya Zhitomirskiy, students at New York University's Courant Institute of Mathematical Sciences.
Bogardus social distance scale	The Bogardus social distance scale is a psychological testing scale created by Emory S. Bogardus to empirically measure people's willingness to participate in social contacts of varying degrees of closeness with members of diverse social groups, such as racial and ethnic groups. The scale asks people the extent to which they would be accepting of each group (a score of 1.00 for a group is taken to indicate no social distance):•As close relatives by marriage (score 1.00)•As my close personal friends (2.00)•As neighbors on the same street (3.00)•As co-workers in the same occupation (4.00)•As citizens in my country (5.00)•As only visitors in my country (6.00)•Would exclude from my country (7.00)

Chapter 10. Ethnicity and Race

CHAPTER HIGHLIGHTS & NOTES: KEY TERMS, PEOPLE, PLACES, CONCEPTS

	The Bogardus social distance scale is a cumulative scale (a Guttman scale), because agreement with any item implies agreement with all preceding items. The scale has been criticized as too simple because the social interactions and attitudes in close familial or friendship-type relationships may be qualitatively different from social interactions with and attitudes toward relationships with far-away contacts such as citizens or visitors in one's country.
Emory S. Bogardus	Emory S. Bogardus was a prominent figure in the history of American sociology. Bogardus founded one of the first sociology departments at an American university, at the University of Southern California in 1915.
Chinese Exclusion Act	The Chinese Exclusion Act was a United States federal law signed by Chester A. Arthur on May 6, 1882, following revisions made in 1880 to the Burlingame Treaty of 1868. Those revisions allowed the U.S. to suspend Chinese immigration, a ban that was intended to last 10 years. This law was repealed by the Magnuson Act on December 17, 1943.
Globalization	Globalization refers to the increasing global relationships of culture, people, and economic activity. It is generally used to refer to economic globalization: the global distribution of the production of goods and services, through reduction of barriers to international trade such as tariffs, export fees, and import quotas and the reduction of restrictions on the movement of capital and on investment. Globalization may contribute to economic growth in developed and developing countries through increased specialization and the principle of comparative advantage.
Black Codes	The Black Codes were laws in the United States after the Civil War with the effect of limiting the basic human rights and civil liberties of blacks. Even though the U.S. constitution originally discriminated against blacks (as 'other people') and both Northern and Southern states had passed discriminatory legislation from the early 19th century, the term Black Codes is used most often to refer to legislation passed by Southern states at the end of the Civil War to control the labor, migration and other activities of newly-freed slaves. In Texas, the Eleventh Legislature produced these codes in 1866, right after the Civil War.
Rosa Parks	Rosa Parks was an African-American civil rights activist, whom the U.S. Congress called 'the first lady of civil rights', and 'the mother of the freedom movement'. On December 1, 1955, in Montgomery, Alabama, Rosa Parks refused to obey bus driver James F. Blake's order that she give up her seat in the colored section to a white passenger, after the white section was filled. Rosa Parks was not the first person to resist bus segregation.

Chapter 10. Ethnicity and Race

CHAPTER HIGHLIGHTS & NOTES: KEY TERMS, PEOPLE, PLACES, CONCEPTS

Civil rights movement	The civil rights movement was a worldwide political movement for equality before the law occurring between approximately 1950 and 1980. In many situations it took the form of campaigns of civil resistance aimed at achieving change by nonviolent forms of resistance. In some situations it was accompanied, or followed, by civil unrest and armed rebellion. The process was long and tenuous in many countries, and many of these movements did not fully achieve their goals although, the efforts of these movements did lead to improvements in the legal rights of previously oppressed groups of people.
Cultural group	The nominal term cultural group generally refers to a self-defined group of people who share a commonality of sociological, ethnographic or regional background experiences which identify them as a group. Cultural groups may be defined by many types of commonality, as such, the method of identification supplies the context for the grouping. ==References==
	A group of people who share common beliefs, value, behavior, these can affect how you relate to other e.g. ethnic (Maori, Pacifier etc), rural urban, youth, beach, sports, religious, hobby etc....
Wealth	Wealth is the abundance of valuable resources or material possessions, or the control of such assets. The word wealth is derived from the old English wela, which is from an Indo-European word stem. An individual, community, region or country that possesses an abundance of such possessions or resources is known as wealthy.
Residential segregation	Residential segregation is the physical separation of two or more groups into different neighborhoods, or a form of segregation that 'sorts population groups into various neighborhood contexts and shapes the living environment at the neighborhood level.' While it has traditionally been associated with racial segregation, it generally refers to any kind of sorting based on some criteria populations (e.g. race, ethnicity, income).
	While overt segregation is illegal in the United States, housing patterns show significant and persistent segregation for certain races and income groups. The history of American social and public policies, like Jim Crow laws and Federal Housing Administration's early redlining policies, set the tone for segregation in housing.
Ghetto	A ghetto is a section of a city occupied by a group who live there especially because of social, economic, or legal pressure. The term ghetto was originally used in Venice to describe the area where Jews were compelled to live. A ghetto is now described as an overcrowded urban area often associated with a specific ethnic or racial population.
Political power	Political power is a type of power held by a group in a society which allows administration of some or all of public resources, including labour, and wealth. There are many ways to obtain possession of such power.

Chapter 10. Ethnicity and Race

CHAPTER HIGHLIGHTS & NOTES: KEY TERMS, PEOPLE, PLACES, CONCEPTS

William Julius Wilson	William Julius Wilson is an American sociologist. He worked at the University of Chicago 1972-1996 before moving to Harvard.
	William Julius Wilson is Lewis P. and Linda L. Geyser University Professor at Harvard University.

CHAPTER QUIZ: KEY TERMS, PEOPLE, PLACES, CONCEPTS

1. _____ refers to the increasing global relationships of culture, people, and economic activity. It is generally used to refer to economic _____: the global distribution of the production of goods and services, through reduction of barriers to international trade such as tariffs, export fees, and import quotas and the reduction of restrictions on the movement of capital and on investment. _____ may contribute to economic growth in developed and developing countries through increased specialization and the principle of comparative advantage.

    a. Historical materialism
    b. Human evolution
    c. Globalization
    d. Kitchin cycle

2. _____, often abbreviated _____ and informally known as The Klan, is the name of three distinct past and present far-right organizations in the United States, which have advocated extremist reactionary currents such as white supremacy, white nationalism, and anti-immigration, historically expressed through terrorism. Since the mid-20th century, the _____ has also been anti-communist. The current manifestation is splintered into several chapters and is classified as a hate group.

    a. The Lambs of Christ
    b. Lombard Street Riot
    c. Los Angeles Jewish Community Center shooting
    d. Ku Klux Klan

3. . _____, 388 U.S. 1 (1967), was a landmark civil rights case in which the United States Supreme Court, by a 9-0 vote, declared Virginia's anti-miscegenation statute, the 'Racial Integrity Act of 1924', unconstitutional, thereby overturning Pace v. Alabama (1883) and ending all race-based legal restrictions on marriage in the United States.

    Facts

Chapter 10. Ethnicity and Race

CHAPTER QUIZ: KEY TERMS, PEOPLE, PLACES, CONCEPTS

The plaintiffs, Mildred Loving (née Mildred Delores Jeter, a woman of African and Rappahannock Native American descent, July 22, 1939 - May 2, 2008) and Richard Perry Loving (a white man, October 29, 1933 - June 1975), were residents of the Commonwealth of Virginia who had been married in June 1958 in the District of Columbia, having left Virginia to evade the Racial Integrity Act, a state law banning marriages between any white person and any non-white person. Upon their return to Caroline County, Virginia, they were charged with violation of the ban.

a. Marabou
b. Mestizo
c. Miscegenation
d. Loving v. Virginia

4. A _____ is the group whose interests a system is meant to serve and whose identity it is meant to represent. The system is a form of government where representatives of a particular group hold a number of posts disproportionately large to the percentage of the total population that the particular group represents and uses them to advance the position of their particular group to the detriment of others.

A group is dominant if it possesses a disproportionate share of societal resources, privileges, and power.

a. Feminism in Egypt
b. Feminist Library
c. Dominant group
d. Feminization

5. _____ is the belief that the genetic factors which constitute race, ethnicity, or nationality are a primary determinant of human traits and capacities and that ethnic differences produce an inherent superiority of a particular race. _____'s effects are called 'racial discrimination.' In the case of institutional _____, certain racial groups may be denied rights or benefits, or receive preferential treatment.

Racial discrimination typically points out taxonomic differences between different groups of people, although anyone may be discriminated against on an ethnic or cultural basis, independently of their somatic differences.

a. Speciesism
b. Racism
c. Left-handedness
d. Legacy preferences

ANSWER KEY
Chapter 10. Ethnicity and Race

1. c
2. d
3. d
4. c
5. b

You can take the complete Chapter Practice Test

for Chapter 10. Ethnicity and Race
on all key terms, persons, places, and concepts.

Online 99 Cents

http://www.epub4.5.21549.10.cram101.com/

Use www.Cram101.com for all your study needs

including Cram101's online interactive problem solving labs in

chemistry, statistics, mathematics, and more.

Chapter 11. Families and Intimate Relationships

CHAPTER OUTLINE: KEY TERMS, PEOPLE, PLACES, CONCEPTS

_____ Extended family

_____ Kinship

_____ Orientation

_____ Polyandry

_____ Polygamy

_____ Polygyny

_____ Betty Friedan

_____ Blended family

_____ Time bind

_____ Clan

_____ Cohabitation

_____ Single-parent

_____ Child abuse

_____ Domestic violence

_____ Margaret Mead

_____ Artificial insemination

Visit Cram101.com for full Practice Exams

Chapter 11. Families and Intimate Relationships

CHAPTER HIGHLIGHTS & NOTES: KEY TERMS, PEOPLE, PLACES, CONCEPTS

Extended family	The term extended family has several distinct meanings. It consists of grandparents, aunts, uncles, and cousins. In some circumstances, the extended family comes to live either with or in place of a member of the nuclear family; a family that includes in one household near relatives in addition to a nuclear family.
Kinship	Kinship is a relationship between any entities that share a genealogical origin, through either biological, cultural, or historical descent. And descent groups, lineages, etc. are treated in their own subsections.
Orientation	Orientation is a function of the mind involving awareness of three dimensions: time, place and person. Problems with orientation lead to disorientation, and can be due to various conditions, from delirium to intoxication. Typically, disorientation is first in time, then in place and finally in person.
Polyandry	Polyandry refers to a form of marriage in which a woman has two or more husbands at the same time. The form of polyandry in which a woman is married to two or more brothers is known as 'fraternal polyandry', and it is believed by many anthropologists to be the most frequently encountered form. Human polyandry According to inscriptions describing the reforms of the Sumerian king Urukagina of Lagash (ca. 2300 BC), he is said to have abolished the former custom of polyandry in his country, on pain of the woman taking multiple husbands being stoned with rocks upon which her crime is written.
Polygamy	Polygamy is a marriage which includes more than two partners. When a man is married to more than one wife at a time, the relationship is called polygyny, and there is no marriage bond between the wives; and when a woman is married to more than one husband at a time, it is called polyandry, and there is no marriage bond between the husbands. If a marriage includes multiple husbands and wives, it can be called group marriage.
Polygyny	Polygyny is a form of marriage in which a man has two or more wives at the same time. In countries where the practice is illegal, the man is referred to as a bigamist or a polygamist. It is distinguished from relationships where a man has a sexual partner outside marriage, such as a concubine, casual sexual partner, paramour, cohabits with a married woman or other culturally but not legally recognized secondary partner.
Betty Friedan	Betty Friedan was an American writer, activist, and feminist.

Chapter 11. Families and Intimate Relationships

CHAPTER HIGHLIGHTS & NOTES: KEY TERMS, PEOPLE, PLACES, CONCEPTS

	A leading figure in the Women's Movement in the United States, her 1963 book The Feminine Mystique is often credited with sparking the 'second wave' of American feminism in the 20th century. In 1966, Friedan founded and was elected the first president of the National Organization for Women, which aimed to bring women 'into the mainstream of American society now [in] fully equal partnership with men'.
Blended family	A stepfamily, also known as a blended family, is a family in which one or both members of the couple have children from a previous relationship. The member of the couple to whom the child is not biologically related is the stepparent, specifically the stepmother or stepfather. The traditional and strictest definition of a 'stepfamily' is a married couple where one or both members of the couple have pre-existing children who live with them.
Time bind	Time bind is a concept introduced by sociologist Arlie Russell Hochschild in 1997 with the publication of her The Time Bind: When Work Becomes Home and Home Becomes Work. This concept refers to the blurring distinction between work and home social environments. Hochschild found in her research that although most working parents, particularly all mothers, said 'family comes first,' few of them considered adjusting their long hours, even when their workplaces offered flextime, paternity leave, telework or other 'family friendly' policies.
Clan	In the African Great Lakes region, the clan is a unit of social organisation. It is the oldest societal structure in the region, other than family and direct lineage. The structure is found in modern-day Rwanda, Burundi, Tanzania and Uganda.
Cohabitation	Cohabitation is an arrangement whereby two people decide to live together on a longterm or permanent basis in an emotionally and/or sexually intimate relationship. The term is most frequently applied to couples who are not married. Reasons for cohabitation Today, cohabitation is a common pattern among people in the Western world.
Single-parent	Single-parents (also lone parent, solo parent and sole parent) is a parent who cares for one or more children without the physical assistance of the other biological parent in the home. 'Single Parenthood' may vary according to the local laws of different nations or regions. Single parenthood may occur for a variety of reasons.
Child abuse	Child abuse is the physical, sexual or emotional mistreatment or neglect of a child or children.

Chapter 11. Families and Intimate Relationships

CHAPTER HIGHLIGHTS & NOTES: KEY TERMS, PEOPLE, PLACES, CONCEPTS

	In the United States, the Centers for Disease Control and Prevention (CDC) and the Department for Children And Families (DCF) define child maltreatment as any act or series of acts of commission or omission by a parent or other caregiver that results in harm, potential for harm, or threat of harm to a child. Child abuse can occur in a child's home, or in the organizations, schools or communities the child interacts with.
Domestic violence	Domestic violence, also known as domestic abuse, spousal abuse, battering, family violence, and intimate partner violence (IPV), is defined as a pattern of abusive behaviors by one partner against another in an intimate relationship such as marriage, dating, family, or cohabitation. Domestic violence, so defined, has many forms, including physical aggression or assault (hitting, kicking, biting, shoving, restraining, slapping, throwing objects), or threats thereof; sexual abuse; emotional abuse; controlling or domineering; intimidation; stalking; passive/covert abuse (e.g., neglect); and economic deprivation. Alcohol consumption and mental illness can be co-morbid with abuse, and present additional challenges in eliminating domestic violence.
Margaret Mead	Margaret Mead was an American cultural anthropologist, who was frequently a featured writer and speaker in the mass media throughout the 1960s and 1970s. She was both a popularizer of the insights of anthropology into modern American and Western culture, and also a respected, if controversial, academic anthropologist. Her reports about the attitudes towards sex in South Pacific and Southeast Asian traditional cultures amply informed the 1960s sexual revolution.
Artificial insemination	Artificial insemination, is the process by which sperm is placed into the reproductive tract of a female for the purpose of impregnating the female by using means other than sexual intercourse or NI. In humans, it is used as assisted reproductive technology, using either sperm from the woman's male partner or sperm from a sperm donor (donor sperm) in cases where the male partner produces no sperm or the woman has no male partner (i.e., single women, lesbians). In cases where donor sperm is used the woman is the gestational and genetic mother of the child produced, and the sperm donor is the genetic or biological father of the child.

Chapter 11. Families and Intimate Relationships

CHAPTER QUIZ: KEY TERMS, PEOPLE, PLACES, CONCEPTS

1. _____ is a function of the mind involving awareness of three dimensions: time, place and person. Problems with _____ lead to dis_____, and can be due to various conditions, from delirium to intoxication. Typically, dis_____ is first in time, then in place and finally in person.

    a. Antonio Commisso
    b. Orientation
    c. Brother-in-law
    d. Cadet

2. _____ refers to a form of marriage in which a woman has two or more husbands at the same time. The form of _____ in which a woman is married to two or more brothers is known as 'fraternal _____', and it is believed by many anthropologists to be the most frequently encountered form.

    Human _____

    According to inscriptions describing the reforms of the Sumerian king Urukagina of Lagash (ca. 2300 BC), he is said to have abolished the former custom of _____ in his country, on pain of the woman taking multiple husbands being stoned with rocks upon which her crime is written.

    a. Polygamy in Christianity
    b. Polyandry
    c. Sister Wife
    d. Bigamy

3. _____ is a marriage which includes more than two partners. When a man is married to more than one wife at a time, the relationship is called polygyny, and there is no marriage bond between the wives; and when a woman is married to more than one husband at a time, it is called polyandry, and there is no marriage bond between the husbands. If a marriage includes multiple husbands and wives, it can be called group marriage.

    a. Polygyny
    b. Polygamy
    c. R/K selection theory
    d. Bigamy

4. The term _____ has several distinct meanings. It consists of grandparents, aunts, uncles, and cousins. In some circumstances, the _____ comes to live either with or in place of a member of the nuclear family; a family that includes in one household near relatives in addition to a nuclear family.

    a. Antonio Commisso
    b. Antonio Imerti
    c. Extended family
    d. Antonio Pelle

Visit Cram101.com for full Practice Exams

Chapter 11. Families and Intimate Relationships

CHAPTER QUIZ: KEY TERMS, PEOPLE, PLACES, CONCEPTS

5. _____ is a relationship between any entities that share a genealogical origin, through either biological, cultural, or historical descent. And descent groups, lineages, etc. are treated in their own subsections.

   a. Babi
   b. Borjigin
   c. Brother-in-law
   d. Kinship

Visit Cram101.com for full Practice Exams

ANSWER KEY
Chapter 11. Families and Intimate Relationships

1. b
2. b
3. b
4. c
5. d

You can take the complete Chapter Practice Test

for Chapter 11. Families and Intimate Relationships
on all key terms, persons, places, and concepts.

Online 99 Cents

http://www.epub4.5.21549.11.cram101.com/

Use www.Cram101.com for all your study needs

including Cram101's online interactive problem solving labs in

chemistry, statistics, mathematics, and more.

Chapter 12. Education and Religion

CHAPTER OUTLINE: KEY TERMS, PEOPLE, PLACES, CONCEPTS

- Homeschooling
- Randall Collins
- Jonathan Kozol
- Internationalization
- Social reproduction
- Hidden curriculum
- No Child Left Behind Act
- Privatization
- Totem
- Secularization
- New religious movement
- Islamic fundamentalism
- Globalization
- Religious nationalism
- Bharatiya Janata Party
- Liberation theology

Visit Cram101.com for full Practice Exams

Chapter 12. Education and Religion

CHAPTER HIGHLIGHTS & NOTES: KEY TERMS, PEOPLE, PLACES, CONCEPTS

Homeschooling	Homeschooling is the education of children at home, typically by parents but sometimes by tutors, rather than in other formal settings of public or private school. Although prior to the introduction of compulsory school attendance laws, most childhood education occurred within the family or community, homeschooling in the modern sense is an alternative in developed countries to private schools outside the home or educational institutions operated by civil governments. Homeschooling is a legal option for parents in some countries to provide their children with a learning environment as an alternative to public or private schools outside the home.
Randall Collins	Randall Collins, Ph.D. is the Dorothy Swaine Thomas Professor in Sociology at the University of Pennsylvania and a member of the Advisory Editors Council of the Social Evolution & History Journal. He is considered to be one of the leading non-Marxist conflict theorists in the United States, •1963 A.B. Harvard College•1964 M.A., Psychology, Stanford University•1969 Ph.D., Sociology, University of California BerkeleyResearch •Sociological Theory•Macro-Historical Sociology of Political and Economic Change•Micro-Sociology: Face-to-Face Interaction•Sociology of Intellectuals (sociology of knowledge)•Social Conflict (Especially Violent Conflict)Writing career Earlier in his academic career, Collins left academia on several occasions to write fiction. One of his novels is The Case of the Philosopher's Ring, featuring Sherlock Holmes.
Jonathan Kozol	Jonathan Kozol is a non-fiction writer, educator, and activist, best known for his books on public education in the United States. Kozol graduated from Noble and Greenough School in 1954, and Harvard University summa cum laude in 1958 with a degree in English Literature. He was awarded a Rhodes Scholarship to Magdalen College, Oxford.
Internationalization	In economics, internationalization has been viewed as a process of increasing involvement of enterprises in international markets, although there is no agreed definition of internationalization or international entrepreneurship. There are several internationalization theories which try to explain why there are international activities. Entrepreneurs/Enterprises Those entrepreneurs who are interested in the field of internationalization of business need to possess the ability to think globally and have an understanding of international cultures.
Social reproduction	Social reproduction is a sociological term referring to processes which sustain or perpetuate characteristics of a given social structure or tradition over a period of time.
Hidden curriculum	A hidden curriculum is a side effect of an education, '[lessons] which are learned but not openly intended' such as the transmission of norms, values, and beliefs conveyed in the classroom and the social environment.

Chapter 12. Education and Religion

CHAPTER HIGHLIGHTS & NOTES: KEY TERMS, PEOPLE, PLACES, CONCEPTS

	Any learning experience may teach unintended lessons. Hidden curriculum often refers to knowledge gained in primary and secondary school settings, usually with a negative connotation where the school strives for equal intellectual development.
No Child Left Behind Act	The No Child Left Behind Act of 2001 (NCLB) is a United States Act of Congress that is a reauthorization of the Elementary and Secondary Education Act, which included Title I, the government's flagship aid program for disadvantaged students. NCLB supports standards-based education reform based on the premise that setting high standards and establishing measurable goals can improve individual outcomes in education. The Act requires states to develop assessments in basic skills.
Privatization	Privatization is the incidence or process of transferring ownership of a business, enterprise, agency or public service from the public sector (the state or government) to the private sector (businesses that operate for a private profit) or to private non-profit organizations. In a broader sense, privatization refers to transfer of any government function to the private sector - including governmental functions like revenue collection and law enforcement. The term 'privatization' also has been used to describe two unrelated transactions.
Totem	A totem is a stipulated ancestor of a group of people, such as a family, clan, group, lineage, or tribe. Totems support larger groups than the individual person. In kinship and descent, if the apical ancestor of a clan is nonhuman, it is called a totem.
Secularization	Secularization is the transformation of a society from close identification with religious values and institutions toward nonreligious values and secular institutions. The secularization thesis refers to the belief that as societies 'progress', particularly through modernization and rationalization, religion loses its authority in all aspects of social life and governance. The term secularization is also used in the context of the lifting of the monastic restrictions from a member of the clergy.
New religious movement	A new religious movement is a religious community or ethical, spiritual, or philosophical group of modern origin, which has a peripheral place within the dominant religious culture. NRMs may be novel in origin or they may be part of a wider religion, such as Christianity, Hinduism or Buddhism, in which case they will be distinct from pre-existing denominations. Scholars studying the sociology of religion have almost unanimously adopted this term as a neutral alternative to the word cult, which is often considered derogatory.

Chapter 12. Education and Religion

CHAPTER HIGHLIGHTS & NOTES: KEY TERMS, PEOPLE, PLACES, CONCEPTS

Islamic fundamentalism	Islamic fundamentalism is a term used to describe religious ideologies seen as advocating a return to the 'fundamentals' of Islam: the Quran and the Sunnah. Definitions of the term vary. According to Christine L. Kettel, it is deemed problematic by those who suggest that Islamic belief requires all Muslims to be fundamentalists, and by others as a term used by outsiders to describe perceived trends within Islam.
Globalization	Globalization refers to the increasing global relationships of culture, people, and economic activity. It is generally used to refer to economic globalization: the global distribution of the production of goods and services, through reduction of barriers to international trade such as tariffs, export fees, and import quotas and the reduction of restrictions on the movement of capital and on investment. Globalization may contribute to economic growth in developed and developing countries through increased specialization and the principle of comparative advantage.
Religious nationalism	Religious nationalism is the relationship of nationalism to a particular religious belief, dogma, or affiliation. This relationship can be broken down into two aspects; the politicisation of religion and the influence of religion on politics. In the former aspect, a shared religion can be seen to contribute to a sense of national unity, a common bond among the citizens of the nation.
Bharatiya Janata Party	The Bharatiya Janata Party is one of the two major political parties in India, the other being the Indian National Congress. Established in 1980, it is India's second largest political party in terms of representation in the parliament and in the various state assemblies. The Bharatiya Janata Party was started by advocating Hindu nationalism and conservative social policies, self-reliance, free market capitalistic policy, foreign policy driven by a nationalist agenda, and strong national defense..
Liberation theology	Liberation theology is a political movement in Christian theology which interprets the teachings of Jesus Christ in terms of a liberation from unjust economic, political, or social conditions. It has been described by proponents as 'an interpretation of Christian faith through the poor's suffering, their struggle and hope, and a critique of society and the Catholic faith and Christianity through the eyes of the poor', and by detractors as Christianized Marxism. Although liberation theology has grown into an international and inter-denominational movement, it began as a movement within the Roman Catholic church in Latin America in the 1950s-1960s.

Chapter 12. Education and Religion

CHAPTER QUIZ: KEY TERMS, PEOPLE, PLACES, CONCEPTS

1. _____ is a term used to describe religious ideologies seen as advocating a return to the 'fundamentals' of Islam: the Quran and the Sunnah. Definitions of the term vary. According to Christine L. Kettel, it is deemed problematic by those who suggest that Islamic belief requires all Muslims to be fundamentalists, and by others as a term used by outsiders to describe perceived trends within Islam.

   a. Islamic inquisition
   b. Islamic revival
   c. Islamic fundamentalism
   d. Islamization

2. _____ is the education of children at home, typically by parents but sometimes by tutors, rather than in other formal settings of public or private school. Although prior to the introduction of compulsory school attendance laws, most childhood education occurred within the family or community, _____ in the modern sense is an alternative in developed countries to private schools outside the home or educational institutions operated by civil governments.

   _____ is a legal option for parents in some countries to provide their children with a learning environment as an alternative to public or private schools outside the home.

   a. social pedagogy
   b. Visa overstay
   c. withdrawl
   d. Homeschooling

3. _____ is the relationship of nationalism to a particular religious belief, dogma, or affiliation. This relationship can be broken down into two aspects; the politicisation of religion and the influence of religion on politics.

   In the former aspect, a shared religion can be seen to contribute to a sense of national unity, a common bond among the citizens of the nation.

   a. Religious nationalism
   b. Reverence
   c. Sanamahism
   d. Secular religion

4. . _____ is the transformation of a society from close identification with religious values and institutions toward nonreligious values and secular institutions. The _____ thesis refers to the belief that as societies 'progress', particularly through modernization and rationalization, religion loses its authority in all aspects of social life and governance. The term _____ is also used in the context of the lifting of the monastic restrictions from a member of the clergy.

   a. Secularization
   b. Totem
   c. Totemism

Visit Cram101.com for full Practice Exams

Chapter 12. Education and Religion

CHAPTER QUIZ: KEY TERMS, PEOPLE, PLACES, CONCEPTS

5. _____, Ph.D. is the Dorothy Swaine Thomas Professor in Sociology at the University of Pennsylvania and a member of the Advisory Editors Council of the Social Evolution & History Journal. He is considered to be one of the leading non-Marxist conflict theorists in the United States, •1963 A.B. Harvard College•1964 M.A., Psychology, Stanford University•1969 Ph.D., Sociology, University of California BerkeleyResearch •Sociological Theory•Macro-Historical Sociology of Political and Economic Change•Micro-Sociology: Face-to-Face Interaction•Sociology of Intellectuals (sociology of knowledge)•Social Conflict (Especially Violent Conflict)Writing career

Earlier in his academic career, Collins left academia on several occasions to write fiction. One of his novels is The Case of the Philosopher's Ring, featuring Sherlock Holmes.

a. Cultural economics
b. Control of fire by early humans
c. Randall Collins
d. Smihula waves

ANSWER KEY
Chapter 12. Education and Religion

1. c
2. d
3. a
4. a
5. c

You can take the complete Chapter Practice Test

for Chapter 12. Education and Religion
on all key terms, persons, places, and concepts.

Online 99 Cents

http://www.epub4.5.21549.12.cram101.com/

Use www.Cram101.com for all your study needs

including Cram101's online interactive problem solving labs in

chemistry, statistics, mathematics, and more.

Chapter 13. Politics and Economic Life

CHAPTER OUTLINE: KEY TERMS, PEOPLE, PLACES, CONCEPTS

_____ | Collective bargaining

_____ | Citizenship

_____ | Sovereignty

_____ | Freedom House

_____ | Minimum wage

_____ | Monarchy

_____ | Social rights

_____ | Welfare state

_____ | Direct democracy

_____ | Participatory

_____ | Participatory democracy

_____ | Communism

_____ | Constitutional monarchy

_____ | Democratization

_____ | Political party

_____ | Proportional representation

_____ | National Organization for Women

_____ | Voter turnout

_____ | Voting behavior

Visit Cram101.com for full Practice Exams

Chapter 13. Politics and Economic Life
CHAPTER OUTLINE: KEY TERMS, PEOPLE, PLACES, CONCEPTS

_____ Political action committee

_____ Roe v. Wade

_____ Power elite

_____ Military budget

_____ War on Terror

_____ Basque nationalism

_____ Islamic fundamentalism

_____ Wealth

_____ Unemployment

_____ Labor union

_____ Capitalism

_____ Corporation

_____ Corporate capitalism

_____ Monopoly

_____ Oligopoly

_____ Welfare capitalism

_____ Senior

_____ Knowledge economy

_____ Knowledge worker

Visit Cram101.com for full Practice Exams

Chapter 13. Politics and Economic Life

CHAPTER OUTLINE: KEY TERMS, PEOPLE, PLACES, CONCEPTS

--------- Contingent workforce

--------- Value chain

--------- John Maynard Keynes

CHAPTER HIGHLIGHTS & NOTES: KEY TERMS, PEOPLE, PLACES, CONCEPTS

Collective bargaining	Collective bargaining is a process of negotiations between employers and the representatives of a unit of employees aimed at reaching agreements which regulate working conditions. Collective agreements usually set out wage scales, working hours, training, health and safety, overtime, grievance mechanisms and rights to participate in workplace or company affairs. The union may negotiate with a single employer (who is typically representing a company's shareholders) or may negotiate with a group of businesses, depending on the country, to reach an industry wide agreement.
Citizenship	Citizenship is the state of being a citizen of a particular social, political, national, or human resource community. The term describing all citizens as a whole is citizenry. In law, citizenship denotes a link between an individual and a state.
Sovereignty	Sovereignty is the quality of having supreme, independent authority over a geographic area, such as a territory. It can be found in a power to rule and make law that rests on a political fact for which no purely legal explanation can be provided. In theoretical terms, the idea of 'sovereignty', historically, from Socrates to Thomas Hobbes, has always necessitated a moral imperative on the entity exercising it.
Freedom House	Freedom House is a nonprofit community-based organization in Roxbury, Massachusetts (a neighborhood of Boston). Freedom House is located in an area sometimes referred to as 'Grove Hall' that lies along Blue Hill Ave. at the border between the Roxbury and Dorchester neighborhoods of Boston.
Minimum wage	A minimum wage is the lowest hourly, daily or monthly remuneration that employers may legally pay to workers. Equivalently, it is the lowest wage at which workers may sell their labour.

Visit Cram101.com for full Practice Exams

Chapter 13. Politics and Economic Life

CHAPTER HIGHLIGHTS & NOTES: KEY TERMS, PEOPLE, PLACES, CONCEPTS

Monarchy	A monarchy is a form of government in which sovereignty is actually or nominally embodied in a single individual (the monarch).
	Forms of monarchy differ widely based on the level of legal autonomy the monarch holds in governance, the method of selection of the monarch, and any predetermined limits on the length of their tenure. When the monarch has no or few legal restraints in state and political matters, it is called an absolute monarchy and is a form of autocracy.
Social rights	Social rights are those rights arising from the social contract, in contrast to natural rights which arise from the natural law, but before the establishment of legal rights by positive law.
	Cecile Fabre argues that 'it is legitimate to constrain democratic majorities, by way of the constitution, to respect and promote those fundamental rights of ours that protect the secure exercise of our autonomy and enable us to achieve well-being. Insofar as, by virtue of Ch. 1, social rights are such fundamental rights, it follows that they should be constitutionalized.'
	From a legal standpoint several approaches exercise and guarantee social rights; social rights under the constitution are rights of subjects or 'subject rights'.
Welfare state	A welfare state is a concept of government where the state plays the primary role in the protection and promotion of the economic and social well-being of its citizens. It is based on the principles of equality of opportunity, equitable distribution of wealth, and public responsibility for those unable to avail themselves of the minimal provisions for a good life. The general term may cover a variety of forms of economic and social organization.
Direct democracy	Direct democracy is a form of government in which people vote on policy initiatives directly, as opposed to a representative democracy in which people vote for representatives who then vote on policy initiatives. Depending on the particular system in use, it might entail passing executive decisions, making laws, directly electing or dismissing officials and conducting trials. Two leading forms of direct democracy are participatory democracy and deliberative democracy.
Participatory	Participation in social science refers to different mechanisms for the public to express opinions - and ideally exert influence - regarding political, economic, management or other social decisions. Participatory decision making can take place along any realm of human social activity, including economic (i.e. participatory economics), political (i.e. participatory democracy or parpolity), management (i.e. participatory management), cultural (i.e. polyculturalism) or familial (i.e. feminism).
	For well-informed participation to occur, it is argued that some version of transparency, e.g. radical transparency, is necessary, but not sufficient.

Chapter 13. Politics and Economic Life

CHAPTER HIGHLIGHTS & NOTES: KEY TERMS, PEOPLE, PLACES, CONCEPTS

Participatory democracy	Participatory democracy is a process emphasizing the broad participation of constituents in the direction and operation of political systems. Etymological roots of democracy imply that the people are in power and thus that all democracies are participatory. However, participatory democracy tends to advocate more involved forms of citizen participation than traditional representative democracy.
Communism	Communism is a sociopolitical movement that aims for a classless and stateless society structured upon common ownership of the means of production, free access to articles of consumption, and the end of wage labour and private property in the means of production and real estate.
	In Marxist theory, communism is a specific stage of historical development that inevitably emerges from the development of the productive forces that leads to a superabundance of material wealth, allowing for distribution based on need and social relations based on freely-associated individuals.
	The exact definition of communism varies, and it is often mistakenly used interchangeably with socialism; however, Marxist theory contends that socialism is just a transitional stage on the way to communism.
Constitutional monarchy	Constitutional monarchy is a form of government in which a monarch acts as head of state within the parameters of a constitution, whether it be a written, uncodified, or blended constitution. This form of government differs from absolute monarchy in which an absolute monarch serves as the source of power in the state and is not legally bound by any constitution and has the powers to regulate his or her respective government.
	Most constitutional monarchies employ a parliamentary system in which the monarch may have strictly ceremonial duties or may have reserve powers, depending on the constitution.
Democratization	Democratization is the transition to a more democratic political regime. It may be the transition from an authoritarian regime to a full democracy, a transition from an authoritarian political system to a semi-democracy or transition from a semi-authoritarian political system to a democratic political system. The outcome may be consolidated (as it was for example in the United Kingdom) or democratization may face frequent reversals (as it has faced for example in Argentina).
Political party	A political party is a political organization that typically seeks to influence government policy, usually by nominating their own candidates and trying to seat them in political office. Parties participate in electoral campaigns, educational outreach or protest actions.

Visit Cram101.com for full Practice Exams

Chapter 13. Politics and Economic Life

CHAPTER HIGHLIGHTS & NOTES: KEY TERMS, PEOPLE, PLACES, CONCEPTS

Proportional representation	Proportional representation is a concept in voting systems used to elect an assembly or council. PR means that the number of seats won by a party or group of candidates is proportionate to the number of votes received. For example, under a PR voting system if 30% of voters support a particular party then roughly 30% of seats will be won by that party.
National Organization for Women	The National Organization for Women is the largest feminist organization in the United States. It was founded in 1966 and has a membership of 500,000 contributing members. The organization consists of 550 chapters in all 50 U.S. states and the District of Columbia.
Voter turnout	Voter turnout is the percentage of eligible voters who cast a ballot in an election. After increasing for many decades, there has been a trend of decreasing voter turnout in most established democracies since the 1960s. In general, low turnout may be due to disenchantment, indifference, or contentment.
Voting behavior	Voting behavior is a form of political behavior. Understanding voters' behavior can explain how and why decisions were made either by public decision-makers, which has been a central concern for political scientists, or by the electorate. To interpret voting behavior both political science and psychology expertise where necessary and therefore the field of political psychology emerged.
Political action committee	In the United States, a political action committee, is the name commonly given to a private group, regardless of size, organized to elect political candidates or to advance the outcome of a political issue or legislation. Legally, what constitutes a 'Political action committee' for purposes of regulation is a matter of state and federal law. Under the Federal Election Campaign Act, an organization becomes a 'political committee' by receiving contributions or making expenditures in excess of $1,000 for the purpose of influencing a federal election.
Roe v. Wade	Roe v. Wade, 410 U.S. 113 (1973), was a landmark controversial decision by the United States Supreme Court on the issue of abortion. The Court decided that a right to privacy under the due process clause in the Fourteenth Amendment to the United States Constitution extends to a woman's decision to have an abortion, but that right must be balanced against the state's two legitimate interests for regulating abortions: protecting prenatal life and protecting the mother's health. Saying that these state interests become stronger over the course of a pregnancy, the Court resolved this balancing test by tying state regulation of abortion to the mother's current trimester of pregnancy.
Power elite	A power elite, in political and sociological theory, is a small group of people who control a disproportionate amount of wealth, privilege, and access to decision-making of global consequence. The term was coined by Charles Wright Mills in his 1956 book, The Power Elite, which describes the relationship between individuals at the pinnacles of political, military, and economic institutions, noting that these people share a common world view.

Visit Cram101.com for full Practice Exams

Chapter 13. Politics and Economic Life

CHAPTER HIGHLIGHTS & NOTES: KEY TERMS, PEOPLE, PLACES, CONCEPTS

Military budget	A military budget also known as a defence budget, is the amount of financial resources dedicated by an entity (most often a nation or a state), to raising and maintaining an armed forces. Military budgets often reflect how much an entity perceives the likelihood of threats against it, or the amount of aggression it wishes to employ. It also provides an idea of how much finances could be provided for the upcoming year.
War on Terror	War on Terror, The Boardgame is a satirical, strategic board game, produced and published in 2006 by TerrorBull Games. War on Terror was originally conceived in 2003 by Andy Tompkins and Andrew Sheerin, two friends based in Cambridge, England. The initial inspiration for the game came from the imminent Invasion of Iraq but, as a whole, was intended as a reaction and challenge to the counter-productive pursuit of the wider War on Terror.
Basque nationalism	Basque nationalism is a political movement advocating for either further political autonomy or, chiefly, full independence of the Basque Country in the wider sense. As a whole, support for Basque nationalism is stronger in the Spanish Basque Autonomous Community and north-west Navarre, whereas in the French Basque Country support is low. Basque nationalism, spanning three different regions in two states is 'irredentist in nature' as it favors political unification of all the Basque-speaking provinces (now divided in those three regions).
Islamic fundamentalism	Islamic fundamentalism is a term used to describe religious ideologies seen as advocating a return to the 'fundamentals' of Islam: the Quran and the Sunnah. Definitions of the term vary. According to Christine L. Kettel, it is deemed problematic by those who suggest that Islamic belief requires all Muslims to be fundamentalists, and by others as a term used by outsiders to describe perceived trends within Islam.
Wealth	Wealth is the abundance of valuable resources or material possessions, or the control of such assets. The word wealth is derived from the old English wela, which is from an Indo-European word stem. An individual, community, region or country that possesses an abundance of such possessions or resources is known as wealthy.
Unemployment	Unemployment, as defined by the International Labour Organization, occurs when people are without jobs and they have actively looked for work within the past four weeks. The unemployment rate is a measure of the prevalence of unemployment and it is calculated as a percentage by dividing the number of unemployed individuals by all individuals currently in the labour force. There remains considerable theoretical debate regarding the causes, consequences and solutions for unemployment.

Chapter 13. Politics and Economic Life

CHAPTER HIGHLIGHTS & NOTES: KEY TERMS, PEOPLE, PLACES, CONCEPTS

Labor union	A labor union is an organization of workers that have banded together to achieve common goals such as better working conditions. The trade union, through its leadership, bargains with the employer on behalf of union members (rank and file members) and negotiates labour contracts (collective bargaining) with employers. This may include the negotiation of wages, work rules, complaint procedures, rules governing hiring, firing and promotion of workers, benefits, workplace safety and policies.
Capitalism	Capitalism is generally considered to be an economic system that is based on the legal ability to make a return on capital. Some have also used the term as a synonym for competitive markets, wage labor, capital accumulation, voluntary exchange, personal finance and greed. The designation is applied to a variety of historical cases, varying in time, geography, politics, and culture.
Corporation	A corporation is an incorporated entity is a separate legal entity that has been incorporated through a legislative or registration process established through legislation. Incorporated entities have legal rights and liabilities that are distinct from its shareholders, and may conduct business for either profit-seeking business or not for profit purposes. Early incorporated entities were established by charter (i.e. by an ad hoc act granted by a monarch or passed by a parliament or legislature).
Corporate capitalism	Corporate capitalism is a term used in social science and economics to describe a capitalist marketplace characterized by the dominance of hierarchical, bureaucratic corporations, which are legally required to pursue profit. A large proportion of the economy and labour market falls within joint stock company or corporate control. In the developed world, corporations dominate the marketplace, comprising 50 percent or more of all businesses.
Monopoly	Monopoly is a board game published by Parker Brothers. he economic concept of monopoly, the domination of a market by a single entity. The history of Monopoly can be traced back to 1904, when an American woman named Elizabeth (Lizzie) J. Magie Phillips created a game through which she hoped to be able to explain the single tax theory of Henry George (it was intended to illustrate the negative aspects of concentrating land in private monopolies).
Oligopoly	An oligopoly is a market form in which a market or industry is dominated by a small number of sellers (oligopolists). Because there are few sellers, each oligopolist is likely to be aware of the actions of the others. The decisions of one firm influence, and are influenced by, the decisions of other firms.

Visit Cram101.com for full Practice Exams

Chapter 13. Politics and Economic Life

CHAPTER HIGHLIGHTS & NOTES: KEY TERMS, PEOPLE, PLACES, CONCEPTS

Welfare capitalism	Welfare capitalism refers either to the combination of a capitalist economic system with a welfare state or, in the American context, to the practice of businesses providing welfare-like services to employees. Welfare capitalism in this second sense, or industrial paternalism, was centered in industries that employed skilled labor and peaked in the mid-20th century. In the 19th century, some companies -- mostly manufacturers -- began offering new benefits for their employees.
Senior	Senior is a term used in the United States to describe a student in the 4th year of study (generally referring to high school or college/university study). High school In the United States, the 12th grade is usually the fourth and final year of a student's high school period and is referred to as senior year. In the England and Wales, anyone in Senior school/ High School (Year 7 - Year 11) an also be known as a senior.
Knowledge economy	The knowledge economy is a term that refers either to an economy of knowledge focused on the production and management of knowledge in the frame of economic constraints, or to a knowledge-based economy. In the second meaning, more frequently used, it refers to the use of knowledge technologies (such as knowledge engineering and knowledge management) to produce economic benefits as well as job creation. The phrase was popularized by Peter Drucker as the title of Chapter 12 in his book The Age of Discontinuity, And, with a footnote in the text, Drucker attributes the phase to economist Fritz Machlup.
Knowledge worker	Knowledge workers are workers whose main capital is knowledge. Typical examples may include software engineers, architects, engineers, scientists and lawyers, because they 'think for a living'. What differentiates knowledge work from other forms of work is its primary task of 'non-routine' problem solving that requires a combination of convergent, divergent, and creative thinking (Reinhardt et al., 2011).
Contingent workforce	A contingent workforce is a provisional group of workers who work for an organization on a non-permanent basis, also known as freelancers, independent professionals, temporary contract workers, independent contractors or consultants. Contingent Workforce Management (CWM) is the strategic approach to managing an organization's contingent workforce in a way that it reduces the company's cost in the management of contingent employees and mitigates the company's risk in employing them.

Chapter 13. Politics and Economic Life

CHAPTER HIGHLIGHTS & NOTES: KEY TERMS, PEOPLE, PLACES, CONCEPTS

	According to the US Bureau of Labor Statistics (BLS), the nontraditional workforce includes 'multiple job holders, contingent and part-time workers, and people in alternative work arrangements.' These workers currently represent a substantial portion of the U.S. workforce, and 'nearly four out of five employers, in establishments of all sizes and industries, use some form of nontraditional staffing.' 'People in alternative work arrangements' includes independent contractors, employees of contract companies, workers who are on call, and temporary workers.
Value chain	The value chain is a concept from business management that was first described and popularized by Michael Porter in his 1985 best-seller, Competitive Advantage: Creating and Sustaining Superior Performance. Firm Level

A value chain is a chain of activities that a firm operating in a specific industry performs in order to deliver something valuable (product or service). A business unit is appropriate level for construction of a value chain, not divisional or corporate level. |
| John Maynard Keynes | John Maynard Keynes was a British economist whose ideas have profoundly affected the theory and practice of modern macroeconomics, and informed the economic policies of governments. He built on and greatly refined earlier work on the causes of business cycles, and is widely considered to be one of the founders of modern macroeconomics and the most influential economist of the 20th century. His ideas are the basis for the school of thought known as John Maynard Keynesian economics, as well as its various offshoots. |

CHAPTER QUIZ: KEY TERMS, PEOPLE, PLACES, CONCEPTS

1. _____ is a concept in voting systems used to elect an assembly or council. PR means that the number of seats won by a party or group of candidates is proportionate to the number of votes received. For example, under a PR voting system if 30% of voters support a particular party then roughly 30% of seats will be won by that party.

    a. Proportional representation
    b. Random ballot
    c. Range voting
    d. Ratings ballot

2. . A _____ is a political organization that typically seeks to influence government policy, usually by nominating their own candidates and trying to seat them in political office. Parties participate in electoral campaigns, educational outreach or protest actions. Parties often espouse an expressed ideology or vision bolstered by a written platform with specific goals, forming a coalition among disparate interests.

Visit Cram101.com for full Practice Exams

Chapter 13. Politics and Economic Life

CHAPTER QUIZ: KEY TERMS, PEOPLE, PLACES, CONCEPTS

a. Precinct captain
b. Preselection
c. Ruling party
d. Political party

3. _____, The Boardgame is a satirical, strategic board game, produced and published in 2006 by TerrorBull Games. _____ was originally conceived in 2003 by Andy Tompkins and Andrew Sheerin, two friends based in Cambridge, England. The initial inspiration for the game came from the imminent Invasion of Iraq but, as a whole, was intended as a reaction and challenge to the counter-productive pursuit of the wider _____.

a. Sons of Iraq
b. War in North-West Pakistan
c. John Yoo
d. War on Terror

4. A _____ is the lowest hourly, daily or monthly remuneration that employers may legally pay to workers. Equivalently, it is the lowest wage at which workers may sell their labour. Although _____ laws are in effect in a great many jurisdictions, there are differences of opinion about the benefits and drawbacks of a _____.

a. Redistribution of wealth
b. Redistributive justice
c. Minimum wage
d. Robin Hood index

5. _____ is a process of negotiations between employers and the representatives of a unit of employees aimed at reaching agreements which regulate working conditions. Collective agreements usually set out wage scales, working hours, training, health and safety, overtime, grievance mechanisms and rights to participate in workplace or company affairs.

The union may negotiate with a single employer (who is typically representing a company's shareholders) or may negotiate with a group of businesses, depending on the country, to reach an industry wide agreement.

a. Community Unionism
b. Collective bargaining
c. Compromise agreement
d. Contractor management

Visit Cram101.com for full Practice Exams

ANSWER KEY
Chapter 13. Politics and Economic Life

1. a
2. d
3. d
4. c
5. b

You can take the complete Chapter Practice Test

for Chapter 13. Politics and Economic Life
on all key terms, persons, places, and concepts.

Online 99 Cents

http://www.epub4.5.21549.13.cram101.com/

Use www.Cram101.com for all your study needs

including Cram101's online interactive problem solving labs in

chemistry, statistics, mathematics, and more.

Chapter 14. The Sociology of the Body: Health, Illness, and Sexuality

CHAPTER OUTLINE: KEY TERMS, PEOPLE, PLACES, CONCEPTS

- Eating disorder
- Famine
- Malnutrition
- Body mass index
- Literacy
- Sick role
- Alternative medicine
- Stigma
- Black Report
- Life expectancy
- World Health Organization
- Hypertension
- Malaria
- Colonialism
- NIE
- Sigmund Freud
- Western culture
- Diversity
- Heterosexuality

Visit Cram101.com for full Practice Exams

Chapter 14. The Sociology of the Body: Health, Illness, and Sexuality

CHAPTER OUTLINE: KEY TERMS, PEOPLE, PLACES, CONCEPTS

- Transvestism
- General Social Survey
- Sexual orientation
- Social network
- Diagnostic and Statistical Manual of Mental Disorders
- Bisexuality
- Homophobia
- Bullying
- Suicide

CHAPTER HIGHLIGHTS & NOTES: KEY TERMS, PEOPLE, PLACES, CONCEPTS

Eating disorder	Eating disorders refer to a group of conditions defined by abnormal eating habits that may involve either insufficient or excessive food intake to the detriment of an individual's physical and mental health. Bulimia nervosa, anorexia nervosa, and binge eating disorder are the most common specific forms in the United Kingdom. Though primarily thought of as affecting females (an estimated 5-10 million being affected in the U.K)., eating disorders affect males as well Template:An estimated 10 - 15% of people with eating disorders are males (Gorgan, 1999).
Famine	A famine is a widespread scarcity of food, caused by several factors including crop failure, overpopulation, or government policies. This phenomenon is usually accompanied or followed by regional malnutrition, starvation, epidemic, and increased mortality. Nearly every continent in the world has experienced a period of famine throughout history.
Malnutrition	Malnutrition is the condition that results from taking an unbalanced diet in which certain nutrients are lacking, in excess (too high an intake), or in the wrong proportions.

Chapter 14. The Sociology of the Body: Health, Illness, and Sexuality

CHAPTER HIGHLIGHTS & NOTES: KEY TERMS, PEOPLE, PLACES, CONCEPTS

	A number of different nutrition disorders may arise, depending on which nutrients are under or overabundant in the diet. In most of the world, malnutrition is present in the form of undernutrition, which is caused by a diet lacking adequate calories and protein.
Body mass index	The body mass index or Quetelet index, is a heuristic proxy for human body fat based on an individual's weight and height. body mass index does not actually measure the percentage of body fat. It was devised between 1830 and 1850 by the Belgian polymath Adolphe Quetelet during the course of developing 'social physics'.
Literacy	Literacy has traditionally been described as the ability to read and write. It is a concept claimed and defined by a range of different theoretical fields. The United Nations Educational, Scientific and Cultural Organization (UNESCO) defines literacy as the 'ability to identify, understand, interpret, create, communicate, compute and use printed and written materials associated with varying contexts.
Sick role	Sick role is a term used in medical sociology concerning the social aspects of falling ill and the privileges and obligations that accompany it. It is a concept created by American sociologist Talcott Parsons in 1951. Concept Parsons was a functionalist sociologist, who argued that being sick means that the sufferer enters a role of 'sanctioned deviance'.
Alternative medicine	Alternative medicine is any of a wide range of health care practices, products and therapies, which typically are not included in the degree courses of established medical schools. Examples include homeopathy, Ayurveda, chiropractic and acupuncture. Complementary medicine is alternative medicine used together with conventional medical treatment, in a belief, not proven by using scientific methods, that it increases the effectiveness, or 'complements', the treatment.
Stigma	Stigma is a 1972 American drama film. It was produced by Charles Moss, while David E. Durston was both the writer and the director. Prominent themes in the film include racism and sexually transmitted disease.
Black Report	The Black report was a 1980 document published by the Department of Health and Social Security (now the Department of Health) in the United Kingdom, which was the report of the expert committee into health inequality chaired by Sir Douglas Black.

Chapter 14. The Sociology of the Body: Health, Illness, and Sexuality

CHAPTER HIGHLIGHTS & NOTES: KEY TERMS, PEOPLE, PLACES, CONCEPTS

	It was demonstrated that although overall health had improved since the introduction of the welfare state, there were widespread health inequalities. It also found that the main cause of these inequalities was economic inequality.
Life expectancy	Life expectancy is the expected (in the statistical sense) number of years of life remaining at a given age. It is denoted by e_x, which means the average number of subsequent years of life for someone now aged x, according to a particular mortality experience. (In technical literature, this symbol means the average number of complete years of life remaining, excluding fractions of a year.
World Health Organization	The World Health Organization is a specialized agency of the United Nations (UN) that acts as a coordinating authority on international public health. Established on April 7, 1948, with headquarters in Geneva, Switzerland, the agency inherited the mandate and resources of its predecessor, the Health Organization, which was an agency of the League of Nations. Constitution and history The World Health Organization's constitution states that its objective 'is the attainment by all people of the highest possible level of health.' Its major task is to combat disease, especially key infectious diseases, and to promote the general health of the people of the world.
Hypertension	Hypertension or high blood pressure, sometimes called arterial hypertension, is a chronic medical condition in which the blood pressure in the arteries is elevated. This requires the heart to work harder than normal to circulate blood through the blood vessels. Blood pressure is summarised by two measurements, systolic and diastolic, which depend on whether the heart muscle is contracting (systole) or relaxed between beats (diastole).
Malaria	Malaria is a mosquito-borne infectious disease of humans caused by eukaryotic protists of the genus Plasmodium. It is widespread in tropical and subtropical regions, including much of Sub-Saharan Africa, Asia and the Americas. The disease results from the multiplication of malaria parasites within red blood cells, causing symptoms that typically include fever and headache, in severe cases progressing to coma, and death.
Colonialism	Colonialism is the establishment, maintenance, acquisition and expansion of colonies in one territory by people from another territory. It is a process whereby the metropole claims sovereignty over the colony, and the social structure, government, and economics of the colony are changed by colonizers from the metropole. Colonialism is a set of unequal relationships between the metropole and the colony and between the colonists and the indigenous population.

Chapter 14. The Sociology of the Body: Health, Illness, and Sexuality

CHAPTER HIGHLIGHTS & NOTES: KEY TERMS, PEOPLE, PLACES, CONCEPTS

NIE	NIE, short for Niepodleglosc ('Independence'), 'NIE' means also 'NO' in Polish - was a Polish anticommunist resistance organisation formed in 1943 in a case of a Soviet occupation of Poland. Its main goal was the struggle against the Soviet Union after 1944. NIE was one of the most well hidden structures of Armia Krajowa, active to 7 May 1945. Its commanders were General Leopold Okulicki and Emil August Fieldorf. One of the first members of the organisation was Witold Pilecki.
Sigmund Freud	Sigmund Freud was an Austrian neurologist who became known as the founding father of psychoanalysis. Freud's parents were poor, but they ensured his education. Freud chose medicine as a career and qualified as a doctor at the University of Vienna, subsequently undertaking research into cerebral palsy, aphasia and microscopic neuroanatomy at the Vienna General Hospital.
Western culture	Western culture, is a term used very broadly to refer to a heritage of social norms, ethical values, traditional customs, religious beliefs, political systems, and specific artifacts and technologies. The term has come to apply to countries whose history is strongly marked by European immigration or settlement, such as the Americas, and Australasia, and is not restricted to Western Europe. Western culture stems from two sources: the Classical Period of the Graeco-Roman era and the influence of Christianity.
Diversity	The 'business case for diversity' stem from the progression of the models of diversity within the workplace since the 1960. The original model for diversity was situated around affirmative action drawing strength from the law and a need to comply with equal employment opportunity objectives. This compliance based model gave rise to the idea that tokenism was the reason an individual was hired into a company when they differed from the dominant group. This primarily included race, ethnicity, and gender.
Heterosexuality	Heterosexuality is romantic or sexual attraction or behavior between persons of opposite sex or gender in the gender binary. As a sexual orientation, heterosexuality refers to 'an enduring pattern of or disposition to experience sexual, affectionate, physical or romantic attractions to persons of the opposite sex'; it also refers to 'an individual's sense of personal and social identity based on those attractions, behaviors expressing them, and membership in a community of others who share them'. The term is usually applied to humans, but it is also observed in all mammals.
Transvestism	Transvestism is the practice of cross-dressing, which is wearing clothing traditionally associated with the opposite sex or gender. Transvestite refers to a person who cross-dresses; however, the word often has additional physical connotations.

Chapter 14. The Sociology of the Body: Health, Illness, and Sexuality

CHAPTER HIGHLIGHTS & NOTES: KEY TERMS, PEOPLE, PLACES, CONCEPTS

General Social Survey	The General Social Survey is a sociological survey used to collect data on demographic characteristics and attitudes of residents of the United States. The survey is conducted face-to-face with an in-person interview by the National Opinion Research Center at the University of Chicago, of a randomly-selected sample of adults (18+) who are not institutionalized. The survey was conducted every year from 1972 to 1994 (except in 1979, 1981, and 1992).
Sexual orientation	Sexual orientation describes an enduring pattern of attraction-emotional, romantic, sexual, or some combination of these-to persons of the opposite sex, the same sex, or to both sexes, as well as the genders that accompany them. These attractions are generally subsumed under heterosexuality, homosexuality, and bisexuality, while asexuality (the lack of romantic or sexual attraction to others) is sometimes identified as the fourth category. These categories are aspects of the more nuanced nature of sexual identity.
Social network	A social network is a social structure made up of a set of actors (such as individuals or organizations) and the dyadic ties between these actors. The social network perspective provides a clear way of analyzing the structure of whole social entities. The study of these structures usessocial network analysis to identify local and global patterns, locate influential entities, and examine network dynamics.
Diagnostic and Statistical Manual of Mental Disorders	The Diagnostic and Statistical Manual of Mental Disorders published by the American Psychiatric Association provides a common language and standard criteria for the classification of mental disorders. It is used in the United States and in varying degrees around the world, by clinicians, researchers, psychiatric drug regulation agencies, health insurance companies, pharmaceutical companies, and policy makers. The current version is the DSM-IV-TR (fourth edition, text revision).
Bisexuality	Bisexuality is sexual behavior or an orientation involving physical or romantic attraction to males and females, especially with regard to men and women. It is one of the three main classifications of sexual orientation, along with a heterosexual and a homosexual orientation, all a part of the heterosexual-homosexual continuum. Pansexuality may or may not be subsumed under bisexuality, with some sources stating that bisexuality encompasses sexual or romantic attraction to all gender identities.
Homophobia	Homophobia encompasses a range of negative attitudes and feelings toward homosexuality or people who are identified or perceived as being lesbian, gay, bisexual or transgender (LGBT). It can be expressed as antipathy, contempt, prejudice, aversion, or hatred, and may be based on irrational fear. Homophobia is observable in critical and hostile behavior such as discrimination and violence on the basis of sexual orientations that are non-heterosexual.

Visit Cram101.com for full Practice Exams

Chapter 14. The Sociology of the Body: Health, Illness, and Sexuality

CHAPTER HIGHLIGHTS & NOTES: KEY TERMS, PEOPLE, PLACES, CONCEPTS

Bullying	Bullying is a form of abuse. It involves repeated acts over time attempting to create or enforce one person's (or group's) power over another person (or group), thus an 'imbalance of power'. The 'imbalance of power' may be social power and/or physical power.
Suicide	Suicide was one of the groundbreaking books in the field of sociology. Written by French sociologist Émile Durkheim and published in 1897 it was a case study (some argue that it is not a case study, and that this is what makes it unique among other scholarly work on the same subject) of suicide, a publication unique for its time which provided an example of what the sociological monograph should look like. Durkheim explores the differing suicide rates among Protestants and Catholics, arguing that stronger social control among Catholics results in lower suicide rates.

CHAPTER QUIZ: KEY TERMS, PEOPLE, PLACES, CONCEPTS

1. _____ encompasses a range of negative attitudes and feelings toward homosexuality or people who are identified or perceived as being lesbian, gay, bisexual or transgender (LGBT). It can be expressed as antipathy, contempt, prejudice, aversion, or hatred, and may be based on irrational fear.

   _____ is observable in critical and hostile behavior such as discrimination and violence on the basis of sexual orientations that are non-heterosexual.

   a. Visa overstay
   b. Homophobia
   c. Chonga
   d. Colonial/Modern Gender System

2. A _____ is a social structure made up of a set of actors (such as individuals or organizations) and the dyadic ties between these actors. The _____ perspective provides a clear way of analyzing the structure of whole social entities. The study of these structures uses_____ analysis to identify local and global patterns, locate influential entities, and examine network dynamics.

   a. Social network
   b. Social rule system theory
   c. Social threefolding
   d. The Sociological Imagination

3. . _____ is the expected (in the statistical sense) number of years of life remaining at a given age.

Chapter 14. The Sociology of the Body: Health, Illness, and Sexuality

CHAPTER QUIZ: KEY TERMS, PEOPLE, PLACES, CONCEPTS

It is denoted by e_x, which means the average number of subsequent years of life for someone now aged x, according to a particular mortality experience. (In technical literature, this symbol means the average number of complete years of life remaining, excluding fractions of a year.

a. Population pyramid
b. Progeria
c. Rejuvenation
d. Life expectancy

4. _____ is a 1972 American drama film. It was produced by Charles Moss, while David E. Durston was both the writer and the director. Prominent themes in the film include racism and sexually transmitted disease.

a. To Kill a Mockingbird
b. Stigma
c. withdrawl
d. Subclinical infection

5. _____ was an Austrian neurologist who became known as the founding father of psychoanalysis.

Freud's parents were poor, but they ensured his education. Freud chose medicine as a career and qualified as a doctor at the University of Vienna, subsequently undertaking research into cerebral palsy, aphasia and microscopic neuroanatomy at the Vienna General Hospital.

a. Philippe Pinel
b. Northern Epirus Liberation Front
c. Sigmund Freud
d. Red Orchestra

Visit Cram101.com for full Practice Exams

ANSWER KEY
Chapter 14. The Sociology of the Body: Health, Illness, and Sexuality

1. b
2. a
3. d
4. b
5. c

You can take the complete Chapter Practice Test

for Chapter 14. The Sociology of the Body: Health, Illness, and Sexuality

on all key terms, persons, places, and concepts.

Online 99 Cents

http://www.epub4.5.21549.14.cram101.com/

Use www.Cram101.com for all your study needs

including Cram101's online interactive problem solving labs in

chemistry, statistics, mathematics, and more.

Chapter 15. Urbanization, Population, and the Environment

CHAPTER OUTLINE: KEY TERMS, PEOPLE, PLACES, CONCEPTS

_____ Environment

_____ Urbanization

_____ Climate change

_____ Global warming

_____ Megalopolis

_____ Ernest Burgess

_____ Chicago school

_____ Robert E. Park

_____ Globalization

_____ Metropolitan area

_____ Population growth

_____ Urban ecology

_____ San Francisco

_____ Urbanism

_____ John Baker

_____ Suburbanization

_____ William Julius Wilson

_____ Gentrification

_____ Residential segregation

Visit Cram101.com for full Practice Exams

Chapter 15. Urbanization, Population, and the Environment

CHAPTER OUTLINE: KEY TERMS, PEOPLE, PLACES, CONCEPTS

_____ | Streetwise

_____ | Urban Renewal

_____ | Global city

_____ | Saskia Sassen

_____ | Megacity

_____ | Birth Control

_____ | Demography

_____ | Fertility

_____ | Infant mortality

_____ | Life expectancy

_____ | Mortality rate

_____ | Malthusianism

_____ | Demographic transition

_____ | Total fertility rate

_____ | Dependency ratio

_____ | Famine

_____ | Biodiversity

_____ | Sustainable development

Chapter 15. Urbanization, Population, and the Environment

CHAPTER HIGHLIGHTS & NOTES: KEY TERMS, PEOPLE, PLACES, CONCEPTS

Environment	The biophysical environment is the biotic and abiotic surrounding of an organism, or population, and includes particularly the factors that have an influence in their survival, development and evolution. The naked term environment can make reference to different concepts, but it is often used as a short form for the biophysical environment. This practice is common, for instance, among governments, that usually name their departments and agencies dealing with the biophysical environment with denominations like Environment Agency.
Urbanization	Urbanization, urbanisation or urban drift is the physical growth of urban areas as a result of rural migration and even suburban concentration into cities, particularly the very largest ones. The United Nations projected that half of the world's population would live in urban areas at the end of 2008. It closely linked to modernization, industrialization, and the sociological process of rationalization.
Climate change	Climate change is a long-term change in the statistical distribution of weather patterns over periods of time that range from decades to millions of years. It may be a change in the average weather conditions or a change in the distribution of weather events with respect to an average, for example, greater or fewer extreme weather events. Climate change may be limited to a specific region, or may occur across the whole Earth.
Global warming	Global warming is the increase in the average temperature of Earth's near-surface air and oceans since the mid-20th century and its projected continuation. According to the 2007 Fourth Assessment Report by the Intergovernmental Panel on Climate Change (IPCC), global surface temperature increased by 0.74 ± 0.18 °C (1.33 ± 0.32 °F) during the 20th century.[A] Most of the observed temperature increase since the middle of the 20th century has been caused by increasing concentrations of greenhouse gases, which result from human activities such as the burning of fossil fuel and deforestation. Climate model projections summarized in the latest IPCC report indicate that the global surface temperature is likely to rise a further 1.1 to 6.4 °C (2.0 to 11.5 °F) during the 21st century.
Megalopolis	A megalopolis (sometimes called a megapolis or megaregion) is typically defined as a chain of roughly adjacent metropolitan areas. The term was used by Oswald Spengler in his 1918 book, The Decline of the West, and Lewis Mumford in his 1938 book, The Culture of Cities, which described it as the first stage in urban overdevelopment and social decline. Later, it was used by Jean Gottmann in 1957, to describe the huge metropolitan area along the eastern seaboard of the U.S. extending from Boston, Massachusetts through New York City; Philadelphia, Pennsylvania; Baltimore, Maryland and ending in Washington, D.C.

Chapter 15. Urbanization, Population, and the Environment

CHAPTER HIGHLIGHTS & NOTES: KEY TERMS, PEOPLE, PLACES, CONCEPTS

Ernest Burgess	Ernest Watson Burgess (May 16, 1886 - December 27, 1966) was an urban sociologist born in Tilbury, Ontario. He was educated at Kingfisher College in Oklahoma and continued graduate studies in sociology at the University of Chicago. In 1916, he returned to the University of Chicago, as a faculty member. Burgess was hired as an urban sociologist at the University of Chicago. Burgess also served as the 24th President of the American Sociological Association (ASA). Five years after his arrival as a professor at the University of a Chicago in 1921, Ernest Burgess would publish one of his most celebrated works.
Chicago school	In sociology and later criminology, the Chicago School was the first major body of works emerging during the 1920s and 1930s specialising in urban sociology, and the research into the urban environment by combining theory and ethnographic fieldwork in Chicago, now applied elsewhere. While involving scholars at several Chicago area universities, the term is often used interchangeably to refer to the University of Chicago's sociology department--one of the oldest and one of the most prestigious. Following World War II, a 'Second Chicago School' arose whose members used symbolic interactionism combined with methods of field research, to create a new body of works.
Robert E. Park	Robert E. Park (February 14, 1864 - February 7, 1944) was an American urban sociologist who is considered to be one of the most influential figures in early U.S. sociology. From 1905 to 1914 Park worked with Booker T. Washington at the Tuskegee Institute. After Tuskegee, he taught at the University of Chicago, from 1914 to 1933, where he played a leading role in the development of the Chicago School of sociology . Park is noted for his work in human ecology, race relations, migration, assimilation, social movements, and social disorganization .
Globalization	Globalization refers to the increasing global relationships of culture, people, and economic activity. It is generally used to refer to economic globalization: the global distribution of the production of goods and services, through reduction of barriers to international trade such as tariffs, export fees, and import quotas and the reduction of restrictions on the movement of capital and on investment. Globalization may contribute to economic growth in developed and developing countries through increased specialization and the principle of comparative advantage.
Metropolitan area	The term metropolitan area refers to a region consisting of a densely populated urban core and its less-populated surrounding territories, sharing industry, infrastructure, and housing. A metropolitan area usually comprises multiple jurisdictions and municipalities: neighborhoods, townships, cities, exurbs, counties, and even states. As social, economic and political institutions have changed, metropolitan areas have become key economic and political regions.

Visit Cram101.com for full Practice Exams

Chapter 15. Urbanization, Population, and the Environment

CHAPTER HIGHLIGHTS & NOTES: KEY TERMS, PEOPLE, PLACES, CONCEPTS

Population growth	Population growth is the change in a population over time, and can be quantified as the change in the number of individuals of any species in a population using 'per unit time' for measurement
	In demography, population growth is used informally for the more specific term population growth rate, and is often used to refer specifically to the growth of the human population of the world.
Urban ecology	Urban ecology is a subfield of ecology which deals with the interaction between organisms in an urban or urbanized community, and their interaction with that community. Urban ecologists study the trees, rivers, wildlife and open spaces found in cities to understand the extent of those resources and the way they are affected by pollution, over-development and other pressures. Analysis of urban settings in the context of ecosystem ecology (looking at the cycling of matter and the flow of energy through the ecosystem) may ultimately help us to design healthier, better managed communities, by understanding what threats the urban environment brings to humans.
San Francisco	'San Francisco' is a song, written by John Phillips of The Mamas & the Papas, and sung by Scott McKenzie. It was written and released in 1967 to promote the Monterey Pop Festival.
	The lyrics of the song tell the listeners, 'If you're going to San Francisco, be sure to wear some flowers in your hair'.
Urbanism	Urbanism is the characteristic way of interaction of inhabitants of towns and cities (urban areas) with the built environment or - in other words - the character of urban life, organization, problems, etc., as well as the study of that character (way), or of the physical needs of urban societies, or city planning. Urbanism is also movement of the population to the urban areas (urbanization) or its concentration in them (degree of urbanization). Theory
	Currently many architects, planners, and sociologists (like Louis Wirth) investigate the way people live in densely populated urban areas from many perspectives including a sociological perspective.
John Baker	John Randal Baker FRS (23 October 1900 - 8 June 1984) was a biologist, physical anthropologist, and professor at the University of Oxford (where he was the Emeritus Reader in Cytology) in the mid-twentieth century. He is best remembered for his 1974 book, Race, which classifies human races in the same way in which animal subspecies are classified. John Baker received his PhD at the University of Oxford in 1927.
Suburbanization	Suburbanization a term used to describe the growth of areas on the fringes of major cities. It is one of the many causes of the increase in urban sprawl.

Chapter 15. Urbanization, Population, and the Environment

CHAPTER HIGHLIGHTS & NOTES: KEY TERMS, PEOPLE, PLACES, CONCEPTS

William Julius Wilson	William Julius Wilson is an American sociologist. He worked at the University of Chicago 1972-1996 before moving to Harvard. William Julius Wilson is Lewis P. and Linda L. Geyser University Professor at Harvard University.
Gentrification	Gentrification and urban gentrification are terms referring to the socio-cultural displacement that results when wealthier people acquire property in low income and working class communities. Consequent to gentrification, the average income increases and average family size decreases in the community, which sometimes results in the eviction of lower-income residents because of increased rents, house prices, and property taxes. This type of population change reduces industrial land use when it is redeveloped for commerce and housing.
Residential segregation	Residential segregation is the physical separation of two or more groups into different neighborhoods, or a form of segregation that 'sorts population groups into various neighborhood contexts and shapes the living environment at the neighborhood level.' While it has traditionally been associated with racial segregation, it generally refers to any kind of sorting based on some criteria populations (e.g. race, ethnicity, income). While overt segregation is illegal in the United States, housing patterns show significant and persistent segregation for certain races and income groups. The history of American social and public policies, like Jim Crow laws and Federal Housing Administration's early redlining policies, set the tone for segregation in housing.
Streetwise	Streetwise may refer to:•Rover Streetwise, a small hatchback made by the MG Rover Group•Knowledge of youth culture, also called 'street'•Practical knowledge, as opposed to ivory tower or book knowledge, knowledge on how to succeed through life, or generally how to avoid the pitfalls•The Streetwise Fund, a mutual fund offered by ING Direct In media•StreetWise, a Chicago newspaper•Street Smarts (game show), a TV game show•Streetwise a 1984 documentary following the lives of homeless teenagers living on the streets of downtown Seattle•Streetwise a 1998 film•Streetwise the name of several Transformers characters.
Urban Renewal	Urban renewal is a program of land redevelopment in areas of moderate to high density urban land use. Renewal has had both successes and failures. Its modern incarnation began in the late 19th century in developed nations and experienced an intense phase in the late 1940s - under the rubric of reconstruction.
Global city	A global city is a city generally considered to be an important node in the global economic system.

Chapter 15. Urbanization, Population, and the Environment

CHAPTER HIGHLIGHTS & NOTES: KEY TERMS, PEOPLE, PLACES, CONCEPTS

	The concept comes from geography and urban studies and rests on the idea that globalization can be understood as largely created, facilitated and enacted in strategic geographic locales according to a hierarchy of importance to the operation of the global system of finance and trade. The most complex of these entities is the 'global city', whereby the linkages binding a city have a direct and tangible effect on global affairs through socio-economic means.
Saskia Sassen	Saskia Sassen is a Dutch-American sociologist noted for her analyses of globalization and international human migration. She currently is Robert S. Lynd Professor of Sociology at Columbia University and Centennial visiting Professor at the London School of Economics. Sassen coined the term global city.
Megacity	A megacity is usually defined as a metropolitan area with a total population in excess of 10 million people. Some definitions also set a minimum level for population density (at least 2,000 persons/square km). A megacity can be a single metropolitan area or two or more metropolitan areas that converge.
Birth Control	Birth Control (also known as The New World) is a 1917 film produced by and starring Margaret Sanger and describing her family planning work. It was the first film banned under a 1915 ruling of the United States Supreme Court that films 'did not constitute free speech'. The banning of 'Birth Control' was upheld by the New York Court of Appeals on the grounds that a film on family planning may be censored 'in the interest of morality, decency, and public safety and welfare'.
Demography	Demography is the statistical study of human populations and sub-populations. It can be a very general science that can be applied to any kind of dynamic human population, that is, one that changes over time or space . It encompasses the study of the size, structure, and distribution of these populations, and spatial and/or temporal changes in them in response to birth, migration, aging and death.
Fertility	Fertility is the natural capability of producing offsprings. As a measure, 'fertility rate' is the number of children born per couple, person or population. Fertility differs from fecundity, which is defined as the potential for reproduction (influenced by gamete production, fertilisation and carrying a pregnancy to term).
Infant mortality	Infant mortality is defined as the number of infant deaths (one year of age or younger) per 1000 live births. Traditionally, the most common cause worldwide was dehydration from diarrhea.

Chapter 15. Urbanization, Population, and the Environment

CHAPTER HIGHLIGHTS & NOTES: KEY TERMS, PEOPLE, PLACES, CONCEPTS

Life expectancy	Life expectancy is the expected (in the statistical sense) number of years of life remaining at a given age. It is denoted by e_x, which means the average number of subsequent years of life for someone now aged x, according to a particular mortality experience. (In technical literature, this symbol means the average number of complete years of life remaining, excluding fractions of a year.
Mortality rate	Mortality rate is a measure of the number of deaths (in general, or due to a specific cause) in a population, scaled to the size of that population, per unit of time. Mortality rate is typically expressed in units of deaths per 1000 individuals per year; thus, a mortality rate of 9.5 (out of 1000) in a population of 1,000 would mean 9.5 deaths per year in that entire population, or 0.95% out of the total. It is distinct from morbidity rate, which refers to the number of individuals in poor health during a given time period (the prevalence rate) or the number of newly appearing cases of the disease per unit of time (incidence rate).
Malthusianism	Malthusianism refers primarily to ideas derived from the political/economic thought of Reverend Thomas Robert Malthus, as laid out initially in his 1798 writings, An Essay on the Principle of Population, which describes how unchecked population growth is exponential (1→2→4→8) while the growth of the food supply was expected to be arithmetical (1→2→3→4). Malthus believed there were two types of 'checks' that could then reduce the population, returning it to a more sustainable level. He believed there were 'preventive' checks such as moral restraints (abstinence, delayed marriage until finances become balanced), and restricting marriage against persons suffering poverty and/or defects.
Demographic transition	Demographic transition refers to the transition from high birth and death rates to low birth and death rates as a country develops from a pre-industrial to an industrialized economic system. This is typically demonstrated through a demographic transition model. The theory is based on an interpretation of demographic history developed in 1929 by the American demographer Warren Thompson (1887-1973).
Total fertility rate	The total fertility rate (TFR, sometimes also called the fertility rate, period total fertility rate or total period fertility rate (TPFR)) of a population is the average number of children that would be born to a woman over her lifetime if•she were to experience the exact current age-specific fertility rates (ASFRs) through her lifetime, and•she were to survive from birth through the end of her reproductive life. It is obtained by summing the single-year age-specific rates at a given time. Parameter characteristics The TFR is a synthetic rate, not based on the fertility of any real group of women since this would involve waiting until they had completed childbearing.

Chapter 15. Urbanization, Population, and the Environment

CHAPTER HIGHLIGHTS & NOTES: KEY TERMS, PEOPLE, PLACES, CONCEPTS

Dependency ratio	In economics and geography the dependency ratio is an age-population ratio of those typically not in the labor force (the dependent part) and those typically in the labor force (the productive part). It is used to measure the pressure on productive population
	In published international statistics, the dependent part usually includes those under the age of 15 and over the age of 64. The productive part makes up the population in between, ages 15 - 64. It is normally expressed as a percentage: $$(Total)\ Dependency\ ratio = \frac{(number\ of\ people\ aged\ 0-14\ and\ those\ aged\ 65\ and\ over)}{number\ of\ people\ aged\ 15-64} \times 100$$
	As the ratio increases there may be an increased burden on the productive part of the population to maintain the upbringing and pensions of the economically dependent. This results in direct impacts on financial expenditures on things like social security, as well as many indirect consequences.
Famine	A famine is a widespread scarcity of food, caused by several factors including crop failure, overpopulation, or government policies. This phenomenon is usually accompanied or followed by regional malnutrition, starvation, epidemic, and increased mortality. Nearly every continent in the world has experienced a period of famine throughout history.
Biodiversity	Biodiversity is the degree of variation of life forms within a given species, ecosystem, biome, or an entire planet. Biodiversity is a measure of the health of ecosystems. Biodiversity is in part a function of climate.
Sustainable development	Sustainable development is a pattern of economic growth in which resource use aims to meet human needs while preserving the environment so that these needs can be met not only in the present, but also for generations to come (sometimes taught as ELF-Environment, Local people, Future). The term 'sustainable development' was used by the Brundtland Commission which coined what has become the most often-quoted definition of sustainable development as development that 'meets the needs of the present without compromising the ability of future generations to meet their own needs.' Alternatively, sustainability educator Michael Thomas Needham referred to 'Sustainable Development' 'as the ability to meet the needs of the present while contributing to the future generations' needs.' There is an additional focus on the present generations responsibility to improve the future generations life by restoring the previous ecosystem damage and resisting to contribute to further ecosystem damage.
	Sustainable development ties together concern for the carrying capacity of natural systems with the social challenges faced by humanity.

Chapter 15. Urbanization, Population, and the Environment

CHAPTER QUIZ: KEY TERMS, PEOPLE, PLACES, CONCEPTS

1. _____ is the physical separation of two or more groups into different neighborhoods, or a form of segregation that 'sorts population groups into various neighborhood contexts and shapes the living environment at the neighborhood level.' While it has traditionally been associated with racial segregation, it generally refers to any kind of sorting based on some criteria populations (e.g. race, ethnicity, income).

   While overt segregation is illegal in the United States, housing patterns show significant and persistent segregation for certain races and income groups. The history of American social and public policies, like Jim Crow laws and Federal Housing Administration's early redlining policies, set the tone for segregation in housing.

   a. Residential segregation
   b. Skid row
   c. Slumlord
   d. Social exclusion

2. Ernest Watson Burgess (May 16, 1886 - December 27, 1966) was an urban sociologist born in Tilbury, Ontario. He was educated at Kingfisher College in Oklahoma and continued graduate studies in sociology at the University of Chicago. In 1916, he returned to the University of Chicago, as a faculty member. Burgess was hired as an urban sociologist at the University of Chicago. Burgess also served as the 24th President of the American Sociological Association (ASA).

   Five years after his arrival as a professor at the University of a Chicago in 1921, _____ would publish one of his most celebrated works.

   a. Karlene Faith
   b. Randall Garrison
   c. Kim Rossmo
   d. Ernest Burgess

3. _____, urbanisation or urban drift is the physical growth of urban areas as a result of rural migration and even suburban concentration into cities, particularly the very largest ones. The United Nations projected that half of the world's population would live in urban areas at the end of 2008.

   It closely linked to modernization, industrialization, and the sociological process of rationalization.

   a. User fee
   b. Anthropocene
   c. Ecocriticism
   d. Urbanization

4. . _____ refers to the increasing global relationships of culture, people, and economic activity. It is generally used to refer to economic _____: the global distribution of the production of goods and services, through reduction of barriers to international trade such as tariffs, export fees, and import quotas and the reduction of restrictions on the movement of capital and on investment. _____ may contribute to economic growth in developed and developing countries through increased specialization and the principle of comparative advantage.

Visit Cram101.com for full Practice Exams

Chapter 15. Urbanization, Population, and the Environment

CHAPTER QUIZ: KEY TERMS, PEOPLE, PLACES, CONCEPTS

   a. Historical materialism
   b. Globalization
   c. Juglar cycle
   d. Kitchin cycle

5. _____ is the increase in the average temperature of Earth's near-surface air and oceans since the mid-20th century and its projected continuation. According to the 2007 Fourth Assessment Report by the Intergovernmental Panel on Climate Change (IPCC), global surface temperature increased by 0.74 ± 0.18 °C (1.33 ± 0.32 °F) during the 20th century.[A] Most of the observed temperature increase since the middle of the 20th century has been caused by increasing concentrations of greenhouse gases, which result from human activities such as the burning of fossil fuel and deforestation.

Climate model projections summarized in the latest IPCC report indicate that the global surface temperature is likely to rise a further 1.1 to 6.4 °C (2.0 to 11.5 °F) during the 21st century.

   a. Government failure
   b. Growth recession
   c. Global warming
   d. Horizontal inequality

ANSWER KEY
Chapter 15. Urbanization, Population, and the Environment

1. a
2. d
3. d
4. b
5. c

You can take the complete Chapter Practice Test

for Chapter 15. Urbanization, Population, and the Environment
on all key terms, persons, places, and concepts.

Online 99 Cents

http://www.epub4.5.21549.15.cram101.com/

Use www.Cram101.com for all your study needs

including Cram101's online interactive problem solving labs in

chemistry, statistics, mathematics, and more.

Visit Cram101.com for full Practice Exams

Chapter 16. Globalization in a Changing World

CHAPTER OUTLINE: KEY TERMS, PEOPLE, PLACES, CONCEPTS

_____ Arab Spring

_____ Libya

_____ Globalization

_____ Social change

_____ Karl Marx

_____ Genocide

_____ William I. Robinson

_____ World Trade Organization

_____ Islamic fundamentalism

_____ Capitalism

_____ Information society

_____ Postmodernism

_____ Social movement

_____ Charles Tilly

_____ Neil Smelser

_____ Collective action

_____ Resource mobilization

_____ Historicity

_____ Social control

Visit Cram101.com for full Practice Exams

Chapter 16. Globalization in a Changing World
CHAPTER OUTLINE: KEY TERMS, PEOPLE, PLACES, CONCEPTS

_____ Social interaction

_____ Civil rights movement

_____ Femininity

_____ Civil society

_____ Information flow

_____ Communism

_____ Amnesty International

_____ Basque nationalism

_____ IGO

_____ Saskia Sassen

_____ Global city

_____ Popular culture

_____ Unemployment

_____ Avatar

_____ External risk

_____ Manufactured risk

_____ Global warming

_____ Global Justice

_____ International Monetary Fund

Visit Cram101.com for full Practice Exams

Chapter 16. Globalization in a Changing World

CHAPTER HIGHLIGHTS & NOTES: KEY TERMS, PEOPLE, PLACES, CONCEPTS

Arab Spring	The Arab Spring is a revolutionary wave of demonstrations and protests occurring in the Arab world that began on Friday, 17 December 2010. To date, rulers have been forced from power in Tunisia, Egypt, Libya, and Yemen; civil uprisings have erupted in Bahrain and Syria; major protests have broken out in Algeria, Iraq, Jordan, Kuwait, and Morocco; and minor protests have occurred in Lebanon, Mauritania, Oman, Saudi Arabia, Sudan, and Western Sahara. Clashes at the borders of Israel in May 2011, as well as protests by the Arab minority in Iranian Khuzestan and a rebellion in Mali have also been inspired by the regional Arab Spring, while the Malian coup d'état has been described as 'fallout'. The protests have shared techniques of mostly civil resistance in sustained campaigns involving strikes, demonstrations, marches, and rallies, as well as the use of social media to organize, communicate, and raise awareness in the face of state attempts at repression and Internet censorship.
Libya	Libya is a country in the Maghreb region of North Africa. Bordered by the Mediterranean Sea to the north, Libya faces Egypt to the east, Sudan to the south east, Chad and Niger to the south, and Algeria and Tunisia to the west. As a result of the 2011 Libyan uprising, there are currently two entities claiming to be the official government of Libya. The regime of Muammar Gaddafi, which refers to the country as the Great Socialist People's Libyan Arab Jamahiriya, controls Tripoli and most of the western half of the country.
Globalization	Globalization refers to the increasing global relationships of culture, people, and economic activity. It is generally used to refer to economic globalization: the global distribution of the production of goods and services, through reduction of barriers to international trade such as tariffs, export fees, and import quotas and the reduction of restrictions on the movement of capital and on investment. Globalization may contribute to economic growth in developed and developing countries through increased specialization and the principle of comparative advantage.
Social change	Social change refers to an alteration in the social order of a society. It may refer to the notion of social progress or sociocultural evolution, the philosophical idea that society moves forward by dialectical or evolutionary means. It may refer to a paradigmatic change in the socio-economic structure, for instance a shift away from feudalism and towards capitalism.
Karl Marx	Karl Heinrich Marx (5 May 1818 - 14 March 1883) was a German philosopher, economist, sociologist, historian, journalist, and revolutionary socialist. His ideas played a significant role in the development of social science and the socialist political movement.

Chapter 16. Globalization in a Changing World

CHAPTER HIGHLIGHTS & NOTES: KEY TERMS, PEOPLE, PLACES, CONCEPTS

He published various books during his lifetime, with the most notable being The Communist Manifesto (1848) and Capital (1867-1894); some of his works were co-written with his friend, the fellow German revolutionary socialist Friedrich Engels.

Born into a wealthy middle class family in Trier, formerly in Prussian Rhineland now called Rhineland-Palatinate, Marx studied at both the University of Bonn and the University of Berlin, where he became interested in the philosophical ideas of the Young Hegelians. In 1836, he became engaged to Jenny von Westphalen, marrying her in 1843. After his studies, he wrote for a radical newspaper in Cologne, and began to work out his theory of dialectical materialism. Moving to Paris in 1843, he began writing for other radical newspapers. He met Engels in Paris, and the two men worked together on a series of books. Exiled to Brussels, he became a leading figure of the Communist League, before moving back to Cologne, where he founded his own newspaper. In 1849 he was exiled again and moved to London together with his wife and children. In London, where the family was reduced to poverty, Marx continued writing and formulating his theories about the nature of society and how he believed it could be improved, as well as campaigning for socialism and becoming a significant figure in the International Workingmen's Association.

Marx's theories about society, economics and politics, which are collectively known as Marxism, hold that all societies progress through the dialectic of class struggle; a conflict between an ownership class which controls production and a lower class which produces the labour for such goods. Heavily critical of the current socio-economic form of society, capitalism, he called it the 'dictatorship of the bourgeoisie', believing it to be run by the wealthy classes purely for their own benefit, and predicted that, like previous socioeconomic systems, it would inevitably produce internal tensions which would lead to its self-destruction and replacement by a new system, socialism. He argued that under socialism society would be governed by the working class in what he called the 'dictatorship of the proletariat', the 'workers state' or 'workers' democracy'. He believed that socialism would, in its turn, eventually be replaced by a stateless, classless society called communism. Along with believing in the inevitability of socialism and communism, Marx actively fought for the former's implementation, arguing that both social theorists and underprivileged people should carry out organised revolutionary action to topple capitalism and bring about socio-economic change.

Revolutionary socialist governments espousing Marxist concepts took power in a variety of countries in the 20th century, leading to the formation of such socialist states as the Soviet Union in 1922 and the People's Republic of China in 1949, while various theoretical variants, such as Leninism, Stalinism, Trotskyism and Maoism, were developed. Marx is typically cited, with Émile Durkheim and Max Weber, as one of the three principal architects of modern social science. Marx has been described as one of the most influential figures in human history, and in a 1999 BBC poll was voted the top 'thinker of the millennium' by people from around the world. Biography Early life: 1818-1835

Chapter 16. Globalization in a Changing World

CHAPTER HIGHLIGHTS & NOTES: KEY TERMS, PEOPLE, PLACES, CONCEPTS

	Karl Heinrich Marx was born on 5 May 1818 at 664 Brückergasse in Trier, a town located in the Kingdom of Prussia's Province of the Lower Rhine. His ancestry was Jewish, with his paternal line having supplied the rabbis of Trier since 1723, a role that had been taken up by his own grandfather, Meier Halevi Marx; Meier's son and Karl's father would be the first in the line to receive a secular education. His maternal grandfather was a Dutch rabbi. Karl's father, Herschel Marx, was middle-class and relatively wealthy: the family owned a number of Moselle vineyards; he converted from Judaism to the Protestant Christian denomination of Lutheranism prior to his son's birth, taking on the German forename of Heinrich over Herschel. In 1815, he began working as an attorney and in 1819 moved his family from a five-room rented apartment into a ten-room property near the Porta Nigra. A man of the Enlightenment, Heinrich Marx was interested in the ideas of the philosophers Immanuel Kant and Voltaire, and took part in agitation for a constitution and reforms in Prussia, which was then governed by an absolute monarchy. Karl's mother, born Henrietta Pressburg, was a Dutch Jew who, unlike her husband, was only semi-literate. She claimed to suffer from 'excessive mother love', devoting much time to her family, and insisting on cleanliness within her home. She was from a prosperous business family. Her family later founded the company Philips Electronics: she was great-aunt to Anton and Gerard Philips, and great-great-aunt to Frits Philips. Her brother, Marx's uncle Benjamin Philips (1830-1900), was a wealthy banker and industrialist, who Karl and Jenny Marx would later often come rely upon for loans, while they were exiled in London. Little is known about Karl Marx's childhood.
Genocide	Genocide is the deliberate and systematic destruction, in whole or in part, of an ethnic, racial, religious, or national group. While a precise definition varies among genocide scholars, a legal definition is found in the 1948 United Nations Convention on the Prevention and Punishment of the Crime of Genocide' The preamble to the CPPCG states that instances of genocide have taken place throughout history, but it was not until Raphael Lemkin coined the term and the prosecution of perpetrators of the Holocaust at the Nuremberg trials that the United Nations agreed to the CPPCG which defined the crime of genocide under international law.
William I. Robinson	William I. Robinson is an American professor of sociology at the University of California, Santa Barbara. His work focuses on political economy, globalization, Latin America and historical materialism. He is a member of the International Parliamentary and Civil Society Mission to Investigate the Political Transition in Iraq.
World Trade Organization	The World Trade Organization is an organization that intends to supervise and liberalize international trade.

Chapter 16. Globalization in a Changing World

CHAPTER HIGHLIGHTS & NOTES: KEY TERMS, PEOPLE, PLACES, CONCEPTS

	The organization officially commenced on January 1, 1995 under the Marrakech Agreement, replacing the General Agreement on Tariffs and Trade (GATT), which commenced in 1948. The organization deals with regulation of trade between participating countries; it provides a framework for negotiating and formalizing trade agreements, and a dispute resolution process aimed at enforcing participants' adherence to World Trade Organization agreements which are signed by representatives of member governments and ratified by their parliaments. Most of the issues that the World Trade Organization focuses on derive from previous trade negotiations, especially from the Uruguay Round (1986-1994).
Islamic fundamentalism	Islamic fundamentalism is a term used to describe religious ideologies seen as advocating a return to the 'fundamentals' of Islam: the Quran and the Sunnah. Definitions of the term vary. According to Christine L. Kettel, it is deemed problematic by those who suggest that Islamic belief requires all Muslims to be fundamentalists, and by others as a term used by outsiders to describe perceived trends within Islam.
Capitalism	Capitalism is generally considered to be an economic system that is based on the legal ability to make a return on capital. Some have also used the term as a synonym for competitive markets, wage labor, capital accumulation, voluntary exchange, personal finance and greed. The designation is applied to a variety of historical cases, varying in time, geography, politics, and culture.
Information society	An information society is a society in which the creation, distribution, diffusion, use, integration and manipulation of information is a significant economic, political, and cultural activity. The knowledge economy is its economic counterpart whereby wealth is created through the economic exploitation of understanding. People that have the means to partake in this form of society are sometimes called digital citizens.
Postmodernism	Postmodernism is a range of conceptual frameworks and ideologies that are defined in opposition to those commonly associated with ideologies of modernity and modernist notions of knowledge and science, such as formalism, materialism, metaphysics, positivism, realism, reductionism, and structuralism. Postmodernism is not a philosophical movement, but rather a number of philosophical and critical methods. In other words, postmodernism is not a method of doing philosophy, but rather a way of approaching traditional ideas and practices in non-traditional ways that deviate from pre-established superstructural modes.
Social movement	Social movements are a type of group action. They are large informal groupings of individuals or organizations which focus on specific political or social issues. In other words, they carry out, resist or undo a social change.
Charles Tilly	Charles Tilly was an American sociologist, political scientist, and historian who wrote on the relationship between politics and society. He was the Joseph L.

Visit Cram101.com for full Practice Exams

Chapter 16. Globalization in a Changing World

CHAPTER HIGHLIGHTS & NOTES: KEY TERMS, PEOPLE, PLACES, CONCEPTS

	Buttenwieser Professor of Social Science at Columbia University.
	Charles Tilly's academic work covered multiple topics in the social sciences and influenced scholarship in disciplines outside of sociology, including history and political science. He is considered a major figure in the development of historical sociology, the early use of quantitative methods in historical analysis, the methodology of event cataloguing, the turn towards relational and social-network modes of inquiry, the development of process- and mechanism-based analysis, as well as the study of: contentious politics, social movements, the history of labor, state formation, revolutions, democratization, inequality, and urban sociology.
Neil Smelser	Neil Smelser's value added theory (or strain theory) argued that six elements were necessary for a particular kind of collective behaviour to emerge:•Structural conduciveness - things that make or allow certain behaviors possible (e.g. spatial proximity)•Structural strain - something (inequality, injustice) must strain society•Generalized belief - explanation; participants have to come to an understanding of what the problem is•Precipitating factors - spark to ignite the flame•Mobilization for action - people need to become organized•Failure of social control - how the authorities react (or don't)
Collective action	Collective action is traditionally defined as any action aiming to improve the group's conditions (such as status or power), which is enacted by a representative of the group. It is a term that has formulations and theories in many areas of the social sciences including psychology, sociology, political science and economics. Social Identity Model of Collection Action
	Researchers Martijn van Zomeren, Tom Postmes, and Russell Spears conducted a meta-analysis of over 180 studies of collective action, in an attempt to integrate three dominant socio-psychological perspectives explaining antecedent conditions to this phenomenon - injustice, efficacy, and identity.
Resource mobilization	Resource mobilization is a major sociological theory in the study of social movements which emerged in the 1970s. It stresses the ability of movement's members to 1) acquire resources and to 2) mobilize people towards accomplishing the movement's goals. In contrast to the traditional collective behaviour theory that views social movements as deviant and irrational, resource mobilization sees them as rational social institutions, created and populated by social actors with a goal of taking a political action.
Historicity	Historicity in philosophy is the underlying concept of history, or the intersection of teleology (the concept and study of progress and purpose), temporality (the concept of time), and historiography (semiotics and history of history). Varying conceptualizations of historicity emphasize linear progress or the repetition or modulation of past events.

Chapter 16. Globalization in a Changing World

CHAPTER HIGHLIGHTS & NOTES: KEY TERMS, PEOPLE, PLACES, CONCEPTS

Social control	Social control refers generally to societal and political mechanisms or processes that regulate individual and group behavior, leading to conformity and compliance to the rules of a given society, state, or social group. Many mechanisms of social control are cross-cultural, if only in the control mechanisms used to prevent the establishment of chaos or anomie. Some theorists, such as Émile Durkheim, refer to this form of control as regulation.
Social interaction	In sociology, social interaction is a dynamic, changing sequence of social actions between individuals (or groups) who modify their actions and reactions due to the actions by their interaction partner(s). Social interactions can be differentiated into accidental, repeated, regular, and regulated. Social interactions form the basis for social relations.
Civil rights movement	The civil rights movement was a worldwide political movement for equality before the law occurring between approximately 1950 and 1980. In many situations it took the form of campaigns of civil resistance aimed at achieving change by nonviolent forms of resistance. In some situations it was accompanied, or followed, by civil unrest and armed rebellion. The process was long and tenuous in many countries, and many of these movements did not fully achieve their goals although, the efforts of these movements did lead to improvements in the legal rights of previously oppressed groups of people.
Femininity	Femininity is the set of female qualities attributed specifically to women and girls by a particular culture. The complement to femininity is masculinity. Feminine attributes These are often associated with life-giving and nurturing qualities of elegance, gentleness, motherhood, birth, intuition, creativity, life-death-rebirth and biological life cycle.
Civil society	Civil society is the arena outside of the family, the state, and the market where people associate to advance common interests. It is sometimes considered to include the family and the private sphere and then referred to as the 'third sector' of society, distinct from government and business. Dictionary.com's 21st Century Lexicon defines civil society as 1) the aggregate of non-governmental organizations and institutions that manifest interests and will of citizens or 2) individuals and organizations in a society which are independent of the government.
Information flow	Information flow in an information theoretical context is the transfer of information from a variable x to a variable y in a given process. Not all flows may be desirable. For example, a system shouldn't leak any secret (partially or not) to public observers.

Chapter 16. Globalization in a Changing World

CHAPTER HIGHLIGHTS & NOTES: KEY TERMS, PEOPLE, PLACES, CONCEPTS

Communism	Communism is a sociopolitical movement that aims for a classless and stateless society structured upon common ownership of the means of production, free access to articles of consumption, and the end of wage labour and private property in the means of production and real estate.
	In Marxist theory, communism is a specific stage of historical development that inevitably emerges from the development of the productive forces that leads to a superabundance of material wealth, allowing for distribution based on need and social relations based on freely-associated individuals.
	The exact definition of communism varies, and it is often mistakenly used interchangeably with socialism; however, Marxist theory contends that socialism is just a transitional stage on the way to communism.
Amnesty International	Amnesty International is a non-governmental organisation focused on human rights with over 3 million members and supporters around the world. The objective of the organisation is 'to conduct research and generate action to prevent and end grave abuses of human rights, and to demand justice for those whose rights have been violated Amnesty draws attention to human rights abuses and campaigns for compliance with international laws and standards.
Basque nationalism	Basque nationalism is a political movement advocating for either further political autonomy or, chiefly, full independence of the Basque Country in the wider sense. As a whole, support for Basque nationalism is stronger in the Spanish Basque Autonomous Community and north-west Navarre, whereas in the French Basque Country support is low.
	Basque nationalism, spanning three different regions in two states is 'irredentist in nature' as it favors political unification of all the Basque-speaking provinces (now divided in those three regions).
IGO	IGO is a Global Positioning System (GPS) navigation software package for personal digital assistants (PDA) and personal navigation assistants (PNA) devices, developed by Hungary-based Nav N Go Kft. Nav N Go iGO is a popular choice for several PNA OEM manufacturers. Products based on the company's navigation software are available worldwide in several leading brands like Asus, Blaupunkt, Clarion, Hewlett-Packard, Nextar, Sony, etc.
Saskia Sassen	Saskia Sassen is a Dutch-American sociologist noted for her analyses of globalization and international human migration. She currently is Robert S. Lynd Professor of Sociology at Columbia University and Centennial visiting Professor at the London School of Economics. Sassen coined the term global city.

Chapter 16. Globalization in a Changing World

CHAPTER HIGHLIGHTS & NOTES: KEY TERMS, PEOPLE, PLACES, CONCEPTS

Global city	A global city is a city generally considered to be an important node in the global economic system. The concept comes from geography and urban studies and rests on the idea that globalization can be understood as largely created, facilitated and enacted in strategic geographic locales according to a hierarchy of importance to the operation of the global system of finance and trade. The most complex of these entities is the 'global city', whereby the linkages binding a city have a direct and tangible effect on global affairs through socio-economic means.
Popular culture	Popular culture is the totality of ideas, perspectives, attitudes, memes, images and other phenomena that are preferred by an informal consensus within the mainstream of a given culture, especially Western culture of the early to mid 20th century and the emerging global mainstream of the late 20th and early 21st century. Heavily influenced by mass media, this collection of ideas permeates the everyday lives of the society. Popular culture is often viewed as being trivial and dumbed-down in order to find consensual acceptance throughout the mainstream.
Unemployment	Unemployment, as defined by the International Labour Organization, occurs when people are without jobs and they have actively looked for work within the past four weeks. The unemployment rate is a measure of the prevalence of unemployment and it is calculated as a percentage by dividing the number of unemployed individuals by all individuals currently in the labour force. There remains considerable theoretical debate regarding the causes, consequences and solutions for unemployment.
Avatar	Avatar is a 2009 American epic science fiction film written and directed by James Cameron, and starring Sam Worthington, Zoe Saldana, Stephen Lang, Michelle Rodriguez, Joel David Moore, Giovanni Ribisi and Sigourney Weaver. The film is set in the mid-22nd century, when humans are mining a precious mineral called unobtanium on Pandora, a lush habitable moon of a gas giant in the Alpha Centauri star system. The expansion of the mining colony threatens the continued existence of a local tribe of Na'vi--a humanoid species indigenous to Pandora.
External risk	External Risks In Contract Law In contract law, are risks that are produced by a non-human source and are beyond human control. They are unexpected but happen regularly enough in a general population to be broadly predictable, and may be the subject of casualty insurance.

Chapter 16. Globalization in a Changing World

CHAPTER HIGHLIGHTS & NOTES: KEY TERMS, PEOPLE, PLACES, CONCEPTS

Manufactured risk	Manufactured risks are risks that are produced by the modernization process, particularly by innovative developments in science and technology. They create risk environments that have little historical reference, and are therefore largely unpredictable. Manufactured risk produces a risk society.
Global warming	Global warming is the increase in the average temperature of Earth's near-surface air and oceans since the mid-20th century and its projected continuation. According to the 2007 Fourth Assessment Report by the Intergovernmental Panel on Climate Change (IPCC), global surface temperature increased by 0.74 ± 0.18 °C (1.33 ± 0.32 °F) during the 20th century.[A] Most of the observed temperature increase since the middle of the 20th century has been caused by increasing concentrations of greenhouse gases, which result from human activities such as the burning of fossil fuel and deforestation. Climate model projections summarized in the latest IPCC report indicate that the global surface temperature is likely to rise a further 1.1 to 6.4 °C (2.0 to 11.5 °F) during the 21st century.
Global Justice	Global Justice is a US-based NGO, founded in 2001 at Harvard University by undergraduate and graduate students. With several different issue campaigns, the organization has chapters on over 15 high school and college campuses across the country. Global Justice's mission is to mobilize students and youth to be activists for a particular form of economic and social justice.
International Monetary Fund	The International Monetary Fund is the intergovernmental organization that oversees the global financial system by following the macroeconomic policies of its member countries, in particular those with an impact on exchange rate and the balance of payments. It is an organization formed with a stated objective of stabilizing international exchange rates and facilitating development through the enforcement of liberalising economic policies on other countries as a condition for loans, restructuring or aid. It also offers loans with varying levels of conditionality, mainly to poorer countries.

Chapter 16. Globalization in a Changing World

CHAPTER QUIZ: KEY TERMS, PEOPLE, PLACES, CONCEPTS

1. The _____ is a revolutionary wave of demonstrations and protests occurring in the Arab world that began on Friday, 17 December 2010. To date, rulers have been forced from power in Tunisia, Egypt, Libya, and Yemen; civil uprisings have erupted in Bahrain and Syria; major protests have broken out in Algeria, Iraq, Jordan, Kuwait, and Morocco; and minor protests have occurred in Lebanon, Mauritania, Oman, Saudi Arabia, Sudan, and Western Sahara. Clashes at the borders of Israel in May 2011, as well as protests by the Arab minority in Iranian Khuzestan and a rebellion in Mali have also been inspired by the regional _____, while the Malian coup d'état has been described as 'fallout'.

   The protests have shared techniques of mostly civil resistance in sustained campaigns involving strikes, demonstrations, marches, and rallies, as well as the use of social media to organize, communicate, and raise awareness in the face of state attempts at repression and Internet censorship.

   a. Arab Spring
   b. Internet in a Suitcase
   c. Internet kill switch
   d. Irrepressible.info

2. _____ is a country in the Maghreb region of North Africa. Bordered by the Mediterranean Sea to the north, _____ faces Egypt to the east, Sudan to the south east, Chad and Niger to the south, and Algeria and Tunisia to the west.

   As a result of the 2011 Libyan uprising, there are currently two entities claiming to be the official government of _____. The regime of Muammar Gaddafi, which refers to the country as the Great Socialist People's Libyan Arab Jamahiriya, controls Tripoli and most of the western half of the country.

   a. Second Spanish Republic
   b. Libya
   c. Visa overstay
   d. Irrepressible.info

3. _____ is an American professor of sociology at the University of California, Santa Barbara. His work focuses on political economy, globalization, Latin America and historical materialism. He is a member of the International Parliamentary and Civil Society Mission to Investigate the Political Transition in Iraq.

   a. William I. Robinson
   b. Captivity of Kodavas at Seringapatam
   c. Captivity of Nairs at Seringapatam
   d. Carthago delenda est

4. . _____ refers to the increasing global relationships of culture, people, and economic activity. It is generally used to refer to economic _____: the global distribution of the production of goods and services, through reduction of barriers to international trade such as tariffs, export fees, and import quotas and the reduction of restrictions on the movement of capital and on investment. _____ may contribute to economic growth in developed and developing countries through increased specialization and the principle of comparative advantage.

Visit Cram101.com for full Practice Exams

Chapter 16. Globalization in a Changing World

CHAPTER QUIZ: KEY TERMS, PEOPLE, PLACES, CONCEPTS

   a. Historical materialism
   b. Human evolution
   c. Globalization
   d. Kitchin cycle

5. The _____ is an organization that intends to supervise and liberalize international trade. The organization officially commenced on January 1, 1995 under the Marrakech Agreement, replacing the General Agreement on Tariffs and Trade (GATT), which commenced in 1948. The organization deals with regulation of trade between participating countries; it provides a framework for negotiating and formalizing trade agreements, and a dispute resolution process aimed at enforcing participants' adherence to _____ agreements which are signed by representatives of member governments and ratified by their parliaments. Most of the issues that the _____ focuses on derive from previous trade negotiations, especially from the Uruguay Round (1986-1994).

   a. World government
   b. World Trade Organization
   c. Caput Mundi
   d. Continental union

ANSWER KEY
Chapter 16. Globalization in a Changing World

1. a
2. b
3. a
4. c
5. b

You can take the complete Chapter Practice Test

for Chapter 16. Globalization in a Changing World
on all key terms, persons, places, and concepts.

Online 99 Cents

http://www.epub4.5.21549.16.cram101.com/

Use www.Cram101.com for all your study needs

including Cram101's online interactive problem solving labs in

chemistry, statistics, mathematics, and more.

Other Cram101 e-Books and Tests

Want More?
Cram101.com...

Cram101.com provides the outlines and highlights of your textbooks, just like this e-StudyGuide, but also gives you the PRACTICE TESTS, and other exclusive study tools for all of your textbooks.

Learn More. *Just click*
http://www.cram101.com/

Other Cram101 e-Books and Tests

Visit Cram101.com for full Practice Exams